GM 4L80E

TRANSMISSIONS

How to Rebuild and Modify

Eric McClellan

CarTech®

CarTech®

CarTech®, Inc.
6118 Main Street
North Branch, MN 55056
Phone: 651-277-1200 or 800-551-4754
Fax: 651-277-1203
www.cartechbooks.com

Edit by Wes Eisenschenk
Layout by Monica Seiberlich

ISBN 978-1-61325-569-8
Item No. SA499

Library of Congress Cataloging-in-Publication Data

Names: McClellan, Eric, author.
Title: GM 4L80E transmissions : rebuild & modify / Eric McClellan.
Description: Forest Lake, MN : CarTech, Inc., [2021] | "No. SA499."
Identifiers: LCCN 2021014345 | ISBN 9781613255698 (paperback)
Subjects: LCSH: General Motors automobiles–Transmission devices,
Automatic–Maintenance and repair.
Classification: LCC TL215.G4 M358 2021 | DDC 629.2/4460288–dc23
LC record available at https://lccn.loc.gov/2021014345

Written, edited, and designed in the U.S.A.
Printed in China
10 9 8 7 6 5 4 3 2

CarTech books may be purchased at a discounted rate in bulk for
resale, events, corporate gifts, or educational purposes. Special
editions may also be created to specification. For details, contact
Special Sales at 6118 Main Street, North Branch, MN 55056 or
by email at sales@cartechbooks.com.

Cover photo courtesy of Monster Transmissions.

A very special thanks to Lonnie Diers of Extreme Automatics for
supplying photos and offering technical support for this book.

DISTRIBUTION BY:

Europe
PGUK
63 Hatton Garden
London EC1N 8LE, England
Phone: 020 7061 1980 • Fax: 020 7242 3725
www.pguk.co.uk

Australia
Renniks Publications Ltd.
3/37-39 Green Street
Banksmeadow, NSW 2109, Australia
Phone: 2 9695 7055 • Fax: 2 9695 7355
www.renniks.com

Canada
Login Canada
300 Saulteaux Crescent
Winnipeg, MB, R3J 3T2 Canada
Phone: 800 665 1148 • Fax: 800 665 0103
www.lb.ca

CONTENTS

DEDICATION

To my wife for putting up with my shenanigans.

ACKNOWLEDGMENTS

I would like to thank Lonnie Diers from Extreme Automatics for his technical assistance; Denny Baierl at Sharadon Performance in Hugo, Minnesota, for showing me the ropes and providing years of expertise and knowledge; Monster Transmission for technical support and material contributions; and Curt Collins at General Motors for his years of constant support with technical knowledge, sharing of data, and ever-present availability.

HISTORY, IDENTIFICATION, AND EVOLUTION

The 4L80E transmission is the successor in a long line of automatic transmissions in the history of General Motors (GM). For the better part of 50 years, GM has been producing highly functional and competent transmissions, and as time progressed, technology followed.

For example, the venerable Turbo Hydra-matic 350 (TH350) 3-speed transmission, which was installed in tens of millions of cars and trucks, was superseded by the 4-speed overdrive 700R4 in 1982. GM wasn't done and morphed it into the 4L60E in 1993 for passenger cars and trucks. With that being said, no one has ever recommended that I (or anyone for that matter) should use a 4L60E for anything other than as a boat anchor, let alone actual use in a vehicle. The "60" is GM's designation for the transmissions load capability of 6,000 pounds.

Likewise, the 4L80E is the generational result of the highly-sought-after TH400. The TH400 was introduced in 1964 and had three forward gears, and, just like the TH350, it has a standard 1:1 final-drive gearset. The 4L80E is a direct evolution of the TH400 and has been integrated with the electronic functions of the 4L60E. The 4L80E even has the word "HYDRA-MATIC." stamped on the passenger's side!

When a good thing works, most companies tend to stick to the theme and not completely reinvent the wheel. (See the full list of vehicles below in which these transmissions can be found). However, the 4L80E was not a GM exclusive—far from it. Rolls-Royce even used the 4L80E in its Silver Spirit Mark II, III, and IV from 1992 to 1998, albeit with some testing and refinements for the dignified posteriors of Rolls-Royce owners. However, the bulk of the transmissions that are out in the wild are designated for heavy-duty work and will be found in heavier GM truck applications.

The major difference in the upgrade from the TH400 to the 4L80E is the use of electronic controls. The 4L80E uses two shift solenoids that were initially called "A & B" but were later renamed "1-2" and "2-3" for compliance with OBDII (on-board diagnostics, version two) standards. The power control module (PCM) activates and deactivates each of these two solenoids in a particular pattern or firing order to achieve the preferred gear ratio.

The combinations and gear ratios look like this:

Combinations		
Gear	**1-2 Solenoid**	**2-3 Solenoid**
First	On	Off
Second	Off	Off
Third	Off	On
Fourth	On	On

Gear Ratios	
Gear	**Ratio**
First	2.48
Second	1.48
Third	1.00
Fourth	0.75

4L80E versus 4L60E

The simplest and most expedient answer as to why someone would choose the 4L80E over the 4L60E is power. The 4L80E is derived from the lauded TH400, and we know how strong that can be. However, the 4L60E is the evolution of the 700R4, which was a fairly basic and entry-level transmission for passenger cars and light-duty trucks beginning in 1982.

The oil pan is also a great way to distinguish a 4L80E from other transmissions. The 4L80E has 17 bolts, which is the most of any GM transmission. The TH350 and TH400 each have 13 bolts, the Powerglide has 14 bolts, and the 700R4, 200R4, and 4L60E have 16 bolts. If you find one with 20 bolts, it is a 6L80E, which

is the successor to the 4L80E. The 4L60E shares the same bolt pattern as the 700R4 and is mostly square, whereas the 4L80E is rectangular with an ear clipped off.

Version Differences

There are a few variations in the life cycle of the 4L80E, but they are mostly divided into two main camps: the older style and the newer style. The variations are easily spotted by even the most novice of builders. The older style is dated 1991 through 1996 and is most noted by the close spacing of the oil cooling lines going in and out of the transmission on the passenger's side.

This placement proved to be quite problematic, as oil could not flow to the middle and rear internal parts of the transmission, which

caused heat-related failures. All subsequent transmissions were changed to have a larger spacing between the two oil lines, which provide better oiling throughout the case. Some older 4L80Es still have the castings in the block, but they are not drilled and tapped to supply oil. The list below provides the variants between model years.

Keep in mind that not all 4L80E components are interchangeable. There have been noticeable changes in some parts from year to year and most will interchange with similar style models. When ordering parts, it's important to know not only what version you have ("early" versus "late") but also what year you are working with, as a few small changes that occurred mid cycle can make a difference.

The intermediate center support for the early and late models of 4L80Es are shown. The early, or 1991–1996 version, is on the left, and the 1997-and-up version is on the right. Notice that the late model has a hole for a seal that allows for lubrication of the gearset, whereas the early version does not, as it is rear oiling. These model-year parts do not interchange.

Identifying Transmissions

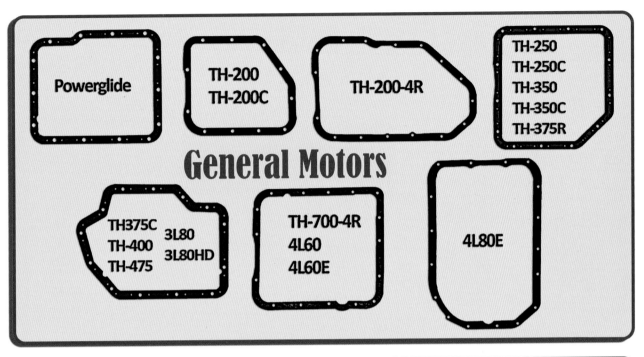

General Motors

Powerglide

TH-200
TH-200C

TH-200-4R

TH-250
TH-250C
TH-350
TH-350C
TH-375R

TH375C
TH-400
TH-475

3L80
3L80HD

TH-700-4R
4L60
4L60E

4L80E

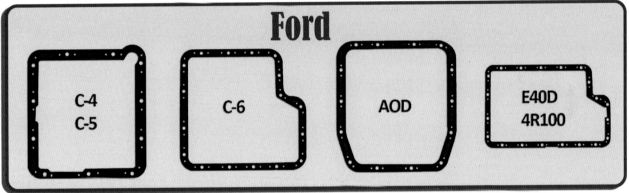

Ford

C-4
C-5

C-6

AOD

E40D
4R100

Chrysler

727/A518

904/A500

Here's a quick identification method if it is not clear by the case. The 4L80E has a brownie-pan shape with one corner clipped off. Of the GM variations, the 4L80E is one of the largest.

RANGE REFERENCE CHART

HYDRAMATIC 4L80-E - GEAR RATIOS

FIRST	2.48	FOURTH	.75
SECOND	1.48	REVERSE	2.08
THIRD	1.00		

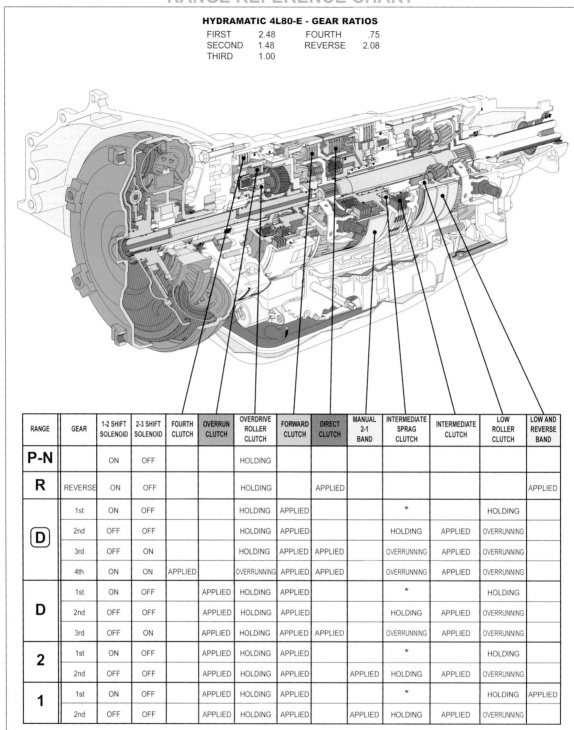

RANGE	GEAR	1-2 SHIFT SOLENOID	2-3 SHIFT SOLENOID	FOURTH CLUTCH	OVERRUN CLUTCH	OVERDRIVE ROLLER CLUTCH	FORWARD CLUTCH	DIRECT CLUTCH	MANUAL 2-1 BAND	INTERMEDIATE SPRAG CLUTCH	INTERMEDIATE CLUTCH	LOW ROLLER CLUTCH	LOW AND REVERSE BAND
P-N		ON	OFF			HOLDING							
R	REVERSE	ON	OFF			HOLDING		APPLIED					APPLIED
Ⓓ	1st	ON	OFF			HOLDING	APPLIED			*		HOLDING	
	2nd	OFF	OFF			HOLDING	APPLIED			HOLDING	APPLIED	OVERRUNNING	
	3rd	OFF	ON			HOLDING	APPLIED	APPLIED		OVERRUNNING	APPLIED	OVERRUNNING	
	4th	ON	ON	APPLIED		OVERRUNNING	APPLIED	APPLIED		OVERRUNNING	APPLIED	OVERRUNNING	
D	1st	ON	OFF	APPLIED	HOLDING		APPLIED			*		HOLDING	
	2nd	OFF	OFF	APPLIED	HOLDING		APPLIED			HOLDING	APPLIED	OVERRUNNING	
	3rd	OFF	ON	APPLIED	HOLDING		APPLIED	APPLIED		OVERRUNNING	APPLIED	OVERRUNNING	
2	1st	ON	OFF	APPLIED	HOLDING		APPLIED			*		HOLDING	
	2nd	OFF	OFF	APPLIED	HOLDING		APPLIED		APPLIED	HOLDING	APPLIED	OVERRUNNING	
1	1st	ON	OFF	APPLIED	HOLDING		APPLIED			*		HOLDING	APPLIED
	2nd	OFF	OFF	APPLIED	HOLDING		APPLIED		APPLIED	HOLDING	APPLIED	OVERRUNNING	

*HOLDING BUT NOT EFFECTIVE

ON = SOLENOID ENERGIZED
OFF = SOLENOID DE-ENERGIZED

@ THE SOLENOID'S STATE FOLLOWS A SHIFT PATTERN WHICH DEPENDS UPON VEHICLE SPEED AND THROTTLE POSTION. IT DOES NOT DEPEND UPON THE SELECTED GEAR.

NOTE: DESCRIPTIONS ABOVE EXPLAIN COMPONENT FUNCTION DURING ACCELERATION.

This chart shows exactly which component is doing what in each condition. (Image Courtesy General Motors)

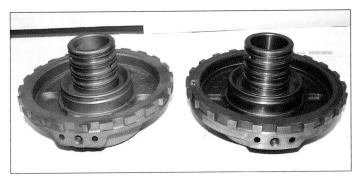

Despite looking very similar from this angle, the early version of the intermediate center support (left) is slightly thinner than its late-model counterpart, which was beefed up to accommodate the extra oiling capacity.

There is a difference between a standard-duty (SD) rear planetary gearset and a heavy-duty (HD) set. The SD set (left) has helical gears, whereas the HD version (right) has straight-cut gears. The straight-cut gears are much stronger and more desirable. These would most likely be found in the heavy-duty applications in the G- or P-style GM vans, such as a big box truck or cab-and-chassis-style trucks. A good way to tell if the 4L80E being removed has straight-cut gears is to look at the underside of the truck and check for a brake drum attached to the transmission. If it does, that's a pretty strong indication that it is an HD version. For high-horsepower or high-towing applications, straight-cut gears are the way to go.

This is a helical gearset that was pulled from a failed transmission. Notice the discoloration on the 12 o'clock gear pin. It should have a gunmetal color like the 2 o'clock pin. This discoloration is a strong indication that the transmission has overheated and died painfully. Also note that the 3 o'clock gear pin and its plastic thrust washer has melted due to the heat. Someone abused this unit. Sadly, it is junk and destined for the recyclers.

Pictured here are two versions of the rear-output carrier assembly. The left side of the image shows the four-wheel-drive (4WD) version, whereas the right is the two-wheel-drive (2WD) carrier. The 2WD carrier has a 40-tooth reluctor ring, and the 4WD carrier has none. The 2WD carrier uses this reluctor ring to the vehicle speed sensor (VSS), while the 4WD variant collects its speed data from the transfer case.

Shown here is a closer view of a straight-cut planetary gearset. Notice that the planetaries are straight as well as the outer ring gear.

Shown here is a complete set of straight-cut gears. For high-horsepower or high-towing loads, this is the gearset for which all the hip and trendy modders are going. This gearset was pulled from a heavy-duty 4L80E at Extreme Automatics in Amelia, Ohio, for a rebuild.

On this complete example of a helical gearset, the sun gears and pins are roasted and failed. It was quite evident that this unit saw either a low-lubrication issue or high-heat situations (or possibly both), which caused its failure. These failures are more common in the early models (1991–1996) than the 1997-and-up versions. This was mainly due to better oiling capacity with the switch from rear oiling to center-feed oiling. The moral of this story and the 4L80E is that either a lack of lubrication (low fluid) or high heat will almost always end in certain death of the unit.

This is another angle of the helical gearset. All of the gears are at an angle and have a slight curve to them.

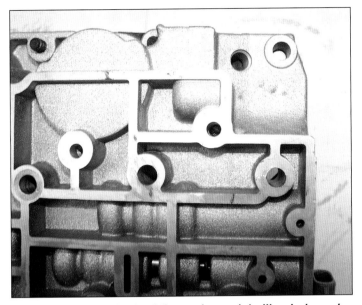

This is a close-up look of the early-model oiling hole and larger-bolt-hole valve body.

The bottom side of the valve bodies between years looks similar. However, this one can be identified as the early model by the rear oiling passage on the bottom left of the spacer plate and valve body.

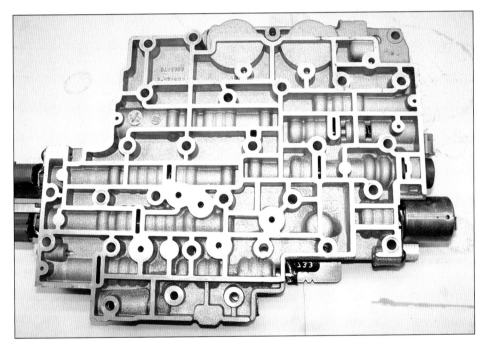

At first glance, the early-model 1991–1996 valve body may be indistinguishable from every other 4L80E valve body. However, look at the upper right corner, where there is a bolt hole with an oil passage for lubrication to flow.

On the side of the valve body is the pressure control solenoid (PCS). This is the two-spaded version used from 1991–1997 and even in a few oddballs through 1999. The old version, commonly called the "tin can" model, should not be reused, as GM has seen a number of failures of this model.

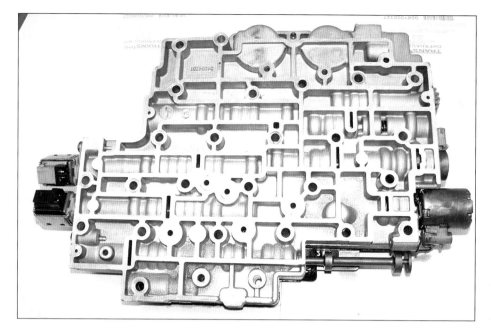

On this 1997-and-up valve body, the upper right does not have a bolt hole or an oiling passage. This was changed due to center gearset oiling over rear-oiling methods.

A close-up view shows that the late-model versions have no bolt or any lubrication passages.

You can identify this valve body for the 4L80E as a late-model version by looking at the bottom left. Note how it does not have a bolt hole or a lubrication passage, as it is blocked off.

Here is the updated PCS from 1997-and-up. Notice that the plug is different, moving from spade to a slip-on weather-pack style. This is why it is important to order the correct wiring harness during rebuilds.

The tab on the 1997-and-up late-model valve body is shown with no bolt hole or oil passage.

This image shows the oiling passage (bottom left) and bolt hole that are not found in the late-model valve body. This indicates clearly that this is an early-model valve body.

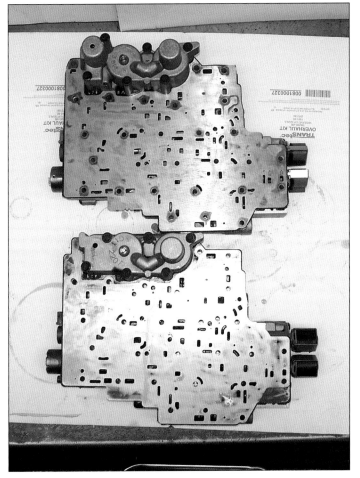

Here is a side-by-side comparison of the early- and late-model valve bodies. The late-model version is shown on top, and the early version is on bottom.

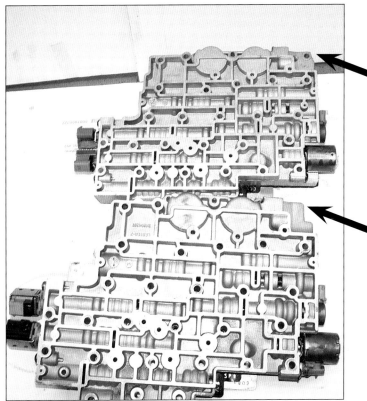

If we flip the valve bodies over, they look virtually identical except for the upper-right tabs. One has oiling capabilities, and one does not. The early versions had the bolt hole and oil hole; the late models do not.

These are the oiling cooling lines for the 1997-and-up 4L80Es. The early models had the cooling lines much closer together, and you can even see the old castings still in the case on the far right.

Look through the case. At the rear is a very small lubrication line on the late-model 4L80Es. On the early cases, the hole will be much larger due to them having a rear instead of center oiling system.

The cases have another difference that is only obvious once the case is opened. In the 12 o'clock position, there is a large reinforcement pin. This pin is found in the 1997-and-up versions and is designed to locate the overdrive pressure plate.

Here is a cleaned-up aluminum 1991–1996 4L80E case. This is most easily identifiable by the forward-most and close-together oiling lines.

Here's the inside of the early-model 4L80E case. Note that at the 12 o'clock position there is not a reinforcement pin for the fourth gear (overdrive gear) pressure plate.

By comparison, the early model of the oiling hole at the rear of the case is much larger, as it required more oil flow due to its rear-oiling system.

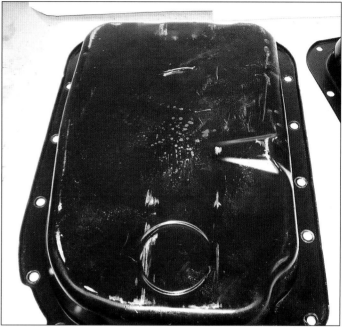

Despite having similar bolt patterns, oil pans do not interchange between early and late models. Pictured here is an early-model 1991–1996 oil pan.

Notice the design change from early to late on this brand-new 1997-and-up oil pan.

The late-model oil pan has a different design and is deeper. The late model holds about a quart more. Despite GM's capacity chart, they are different.

Here are two versions of the fourth gear clutch housing (also called the overdrive clutch housing). This holds the overrun clutches. While appearing similar, they have distinct differences. The fourth clutch housing holds overrun roller clutches. The right housing is the 1997-and-up, and pictured left is the 1991–1996.

1991–1996

This is known to be the "early" style of builds for the 4L80E. These versions are roughly the same from 1991 through 1996. They are known to have poor plastic wiring harnesses and are prone to leaking. While the wiring harness is not a major job to replace while it is installed the vehicle, at bare minimum, it should be replaced when doing any rebuild.

Oil Lubrication

The 1991–1996 models also have the early style of oil lubrication, which is also referred to as a rear-supply style of lubrication. This is where both cooling lines are directly behind the bellhousing in close proximity to one another.

This was a particularly poor design because it caused poor oiling (lubrication) to the rear of the case, which resulted in premature failure. This design also resulted in many case and component differences between these models and the 1997-and-up versions that are known as "late" models.

Shown here are the two available output shafts for the 4L80E from 1991–1996. The 2WD output shaft (left), and 4WD shaft (right) are pictured. The left side has a large hole running through the center because that is how the early 1991–1996 versions lubricated the gearset (rear oiling).

Here are the two output shafts for all 1997-and-up 4L80E variants. The 2WD output shaft (left) and the 4WD version (right) are shown. Notice the hole at the top of the 2WD version, as all 2WD 4L80Es have a bolt-on yoke. These cases also switched from rear-gearset oiling to center-gearset oiling.

Oil Lubrication Holes and Flow Direction		
Fitting Location	**Thread Size**	**Direction of Flow**
Upper	1/4–NPSM	Return/in
Lower	1/4–NPSM	Feed/out

Overdrive Roller Clutch

These models have a larger overdrive roller clutch that typically comes with a 16-sprag element but was updated in later years to have a stronger 34-sprag element. In this instance, the so-called upgrade that was performed by GM to a new overdrive roller clutch bearing was actually a step backward. The early 1991–1996 transmissions had a much stronger overdrive roller clutch bearing compared to the late model, which has smaller bearings and a much smaller overall footprint and surface area.

Bellhousing Bolt Pattern

The early models have the traditional small-block and big-block Chevrolet bellhousing bolt pattern. This means that if you plan to use this version with an LS-style variant, a spacer (GM part number 12563532) and an LS flexplate (GM part number 19260102) will be needed due to the LS family of engines having a shorter crankshaft.

Neutral Safety Switch

These years of the 4L80E do not have the mounting holes for a manual level position switch (MLPS), which is also called the neutral safety switch.

Rear-Style Lubrication System

The early model years of the 4L80E have what is referred to as a rear-style lubrication system. This means that oil is fed from the rear of the case to the front, which proved to be problematic in terms of heat and low-fluid situations. These early versions had a number of unique parts, such as the rear output shaft, crossover tube, center shaft, and rear plug—just to name a few.

1994–1996

The period between 1994 and 1996 had a minor mid-model change, but it falls within the early period. These model variations still hold the small-block and big-block Chevrolet bolt pattern and still retain the early-style lubrication port holes.

EPC Solenoid

The biggest change between the 1991–1996 and the 1994–1996 periods was the upgrade of the electronic pressure control (EPC) solenoid. Many also had a longer shaft for the MLPS.

1997–1999

This short period between 1997 and 1999 had only one major change: the late-model style of lubrication. This moved an oil cooler line from the front-most portion of the transmission to the rear (much farther back) to provide more cooling to the rear of the case. This would provide better lubrication for the entire assembly and better cooling throughout the unit, as heat is the number-one killer of the 4L80E.

Bolt Pattern

Just like the previous years starting in 1991, the 1997–1999 versions kept the small-block and big-block Chevrolet bellhousing bolt pattern intact. Despite the first LS-engine variant debuting in 1997 with the 5.3-liter LS1 in the C5 Corvette, the 4L80E found itself wedged behind truck motors. The truck motors did not see the first LS transplant until 1999, when the LQ4 was introduced (also known as the Vortec 6000). This is why the 4L80E did not see the jump to the LS configuration until the year 2000.

The feed and return lines for the late-model cases are the same fitting size and type.

2000–2003

In the 2000–2003 4L80E model years, the internals stayed virtually identical to the 1997–1999 variant but saw a bellhousing bolt-pattern shift to the LS style. This style uses the same bolt hole locations and alignment pins but adds another bolt hole at the 12 o'clock position of the bellhousing.

If you mate an older-style 4L80E to an LS variation, it will need to use LS bolts, which are metric (M10 x 1.5 x 35 mm), whereas the original small/big-blocks prior to the LS update used US (38-16 x 138).

Oil Flow Direction		
Fitting Location	**Thread Size**	**Direction of Flow**
Front	1/4–NPSM	Feed/out
Rear	1/4–NPSM	Return/in

The 2000-and-newer 4L80E transmission sports a center-high bolt hole to mate to the LS family of engines. The older versions do not have this, which makes it another way to identify the version without having to decode the identification tag.

The tailshaft is 3 inches long, which indicates that this was pulled from a 4WD vehicle. This is neither good nor bad. It only means that we will have to plan accordingly when we put this into another vehicle because the respective configuration may not be suitable.

2004-and-Up

From 2003, the 4L80E saw only small changes except for one. This low number of changes reflects that GM was satisfied with the unit's components and failure rate. There were a few minor valve body changes, but nothing that would cause alarm or change any noticeable characteristics of the transmission.

The one major difference between the 2004 4L80E units and older pre-2004 versions regards the back half of the oil pump. The 2004 back half of the oil pump received a design update. Look carefully at the seal side of the rear half of the pump; there is a small square recess in the pump adjacent to the valve guide. This square recess has an oil passage running through it with what appears to be a small pressure relief cut into the side, which allows fluid to pass from this chamber to another.

This change was significant enough for parts manufacturers to

Shown here is the late-model overdrive clutch housing. At the base of the neck, there is what looks like a groove for a snap ring. Here is how to easily differentiate the two versions: the early model does not have these ring grooves.

When compared to the late-model overdrive clutch housing, this early-model version shows no snap ring groove at the base.

These are the two varieties of roller clutches in the 4L80E. The roller bearing with the blue cage (top) is the late model, which is found in 1997-and-up units. The roller bearing with the black cage (bottom) is the early model that is found in all 1991–1996 4L80Es. The additional surface area for the bearings on the early model makes it stronger than the late model. Unfortunately, these cannot be interchanged.

Another small but significant difference between the model years is this small, square port with a minuscule line to bleed oil pressure next to the valve. This little change was made to 2004-and-up 4L80Es. So, be aware that even though most 1997-and-up variants can interchange most parts, the rear half of the oil-pump unit is not one of them. The oil bleed allows for oil to be bled off (as the name suggests) in an over-pressurization situation. This adds to the life of the pump and will not blow out the seals prematurely.

Here is the pre-2004 rear oil pump half for comparison. It does not have oil square or small bleed-off port. All 2004-and-newer oil pumps cannot be used with any case before 2004. They do not interchange.

Our second (and much older) 4L80E, which was built in 1992, was not cleaned because it only serves as a model to showcase the differences between the older case and newer case. The first and most obvious difference is the placement of the transmission cooling lines. This is the fastest and easiest way to differentiate between a 1991–1996 4L80E and a newer, more desirable version made in and after 1997.

Notice the placement of the oil cooler lines on the early version: close together and near the front of the case.

The older style does have the same style bolt-on driveshaft and interchange with newer versions. This one is from a 4WD version, which can be deduced by the ultra-short tailshaft.

The bellhousing is missing the top bolt hole for the LS family of engines, which was not added until the year 2000. While these can still bolt up to a non-LS engine—you have to love GM for not messing with the engine/transmission bolt pattern—you will be missing the top bolt hole for an LS.

Both versions are identical from the top, except for the upper bolt hole for the engine mount and the cooling lines on the passenger's side. Keep in mind that some versions will still have the cooling lines cast into the case but never drilled, so it is possible to see the old cooling lines in newer versions; they'll just be plugged.

ask builders to specify the year of their case because, according to the parts catalogs that we reviewed, they make a distinct cutoff during that year for this reason.

Basic Information

To gather the necessary images for this project, we snagged two 4L80E transmissions to highlight the differences between the two models. While there are some small iterations in the late models, most parts will

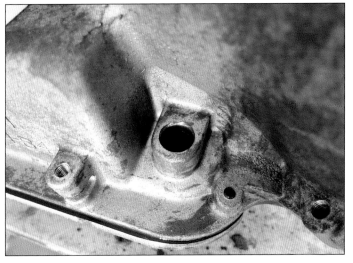

This hole is the dipstick tube and will have a replaceable rubber boot gasket mounted from the inside. A typical rebuild kit will supply one.

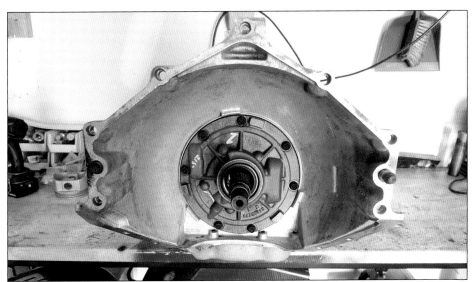

The oil pump side of our donor 4L80E is shown after being cleaned.

The shifter stud sticks out from the driver's side of the transmission. Just behind the stud is the captured bracket that is held in by a special, long pan bolt. It will hold the shifter lever firm to the transmission. The shifter lever is also known as a PRNDL switch, which is used in a majority of vehicles.

This is the electrical connector to drive the transmission. It is removed from the inside of the case and is connected to a series of solenoids that control shift points and perform other functions.

These two large holes on the driver's side serve as holes for critical transmission information. The rear-most hole is the output-shaft speed sensor, which is used for vehicle speed. The front-most hole is the input-shaft or turbine-speed sensor.

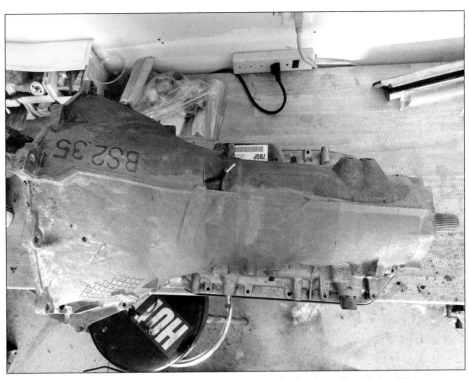

The rear of the case has the tailshaft with a series of six bolts. The 4L80E has a number of different lengths, depending on the vehicle in which it was installed. Most versions are a bolt-on version. The hot rodders out there will need a short tailhousing with a longer tailshaft that will accept a slip-on TH400 yolk.

The only notable fact about the top of the case is the breather tube. The factory has a rubber tube that leads away from hot parts, but most leave this uncapped and without an extension tube.

While it may not look like much, this little O-ring on the input shaft of both versions will impede you from fully disassembling the front oil pump. We learned the hard way that it needs to be removed, no matter how unformidable it may appear.

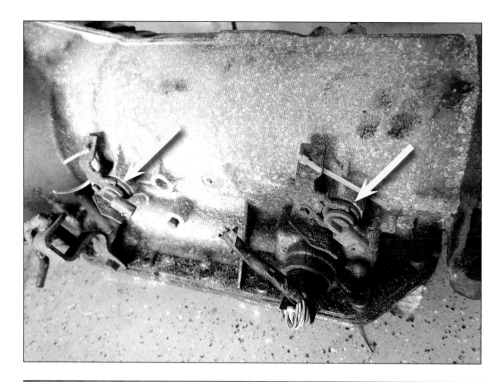

This version came with the input- and output-shaft speed sensors still intact along with the pigtail for the wiring harness and shift cable bracket. Neat.

The wiring harness plugs into the transmission via this port. Do not shove the wiring harness into the port. Otherwise, you risk bending one of the prongs on the receiving end, and repairing that while it is installed on the vehicle would not be pleasant.

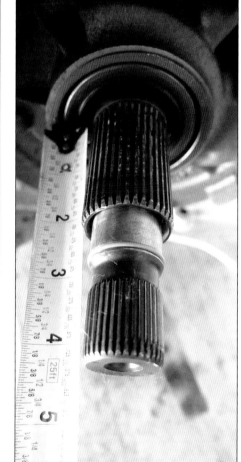

The input shaft measures 4.125 inches and will be covered by the torque converter. Always seat the torque converter properly before installation.

The total width at the widest points (the ears on the lower-most engine bolt holes) measures in at 18.75 inches. Total height from the pan to the upper bolt hole is 18.125 inches.

Fluid Capacities

Please note that these are stock numbers and any aftermarket coolers or lines may add to these overall numbers.

Fluid	Capacity
Total oil capacity	14 to 14.5 liters
Torque converter fill	2.0 liters (approximate)
Oil pan and filter change	4.0 liters (approximate, filled through dipstick tube)
Initial pour	7.7 liters

Dimensions

Aspect	Measurement
Width	20 inches
Length: Standard 2WD	$32^{11}/_{16}$ inches
Length: Heavy-duty (2WD)	$31^{11}/_{16}$ inches
Length: Heavy-duty (long version)	33 inches
Length: 4WD	29 inches (measured to end of case)
Height	$18^1/_4$ inches tall
Tunnel height	$11^1/_2$ inches
Stock torque capacity	440 ft-lbs
Dry weight with converter	254 pounds
Wet weight with converter	268 pounds

interchange except where noted. It should be assumed that early and late editions should not share parts, especially when it comes to components that are noted with oil passages.

Fluid Type

GM recommends a fluid fill of Dexron III. For more-demanding applications, such as towing or plowing, a fill of Dexron VI is highly suggested. Many opt for the Dexron VI on every filter and oil change and every fluid flush just as good insur-

The middle height of the transmission is being measured because we know that many of these units have been rebuilt and installed into cars for which they were never meant. Before modifying the transmission tunnel, the middle height is about 11 inches in total height.

The 4L80E has a very distinct bolt pattern from the bottom. There are 17 holes, and versions will generally be found with only 16 bolts installed. The missing bolt seen here is for the shifter linkage that is captured by a longer bolt than the rest of the group.

ance. This is a good motto: oil may be expensive, but it's not nearly as expensive as a transmission rebuild.

Buyer's Guide

There's a lot of good news when it comes to finding and sourcing a 4L80E. The 4L80E was installed in many GM vehicles over a number of decades. This means that there are literally millions of these just waiting to be bought put back into service. With the high volume comes low entry costs. However, that doesn't mean that the 4L80E wasn't a GM vehicle rarity. The following is a list of vehicles in which the 4L80E transmission was installed. A few might surprise you.

- 1991–2013 Chevrolet C/K/Chevrolet Silverado/GMC Sierra V-8
- 1991–2013 Chevrolet/GMC Suburban/GMC Yukon
- 1995–2003 Chevrolet Tahoe/GMC Yukon
- 1991–2009 Chevrolet Van/Chevrolet Express/GMC Savana
- 2002–2006 Chevrolet Avalanche 8.1L
- 1992–2006 Hummer H1
- 1992–1998 Rolls-Royce Silver Spirit/Spur II, III, IV
- 1991–1992 Bentley Eight
- 1991–1997 Bentley Turbo R
- 1991–2002 Bentley Continental R/S/T
- 1999–2006 Bentley Arnage Red Label/Bentley Arnage R/RL/T
- 1993–1996 Jaguar XJS
- 1994–1997 Jaguar XJR

- 1993–1997 Jaguar XJ12/Daimler Double Six
- 1996–1999 Aston Martin DB7
- 2000–2006 Chevrolet heavy-duty trucks

Being that the 4L80E was a direct descendent of the mighty TH400 and had proven itself to be quite robust, other manufacturers were keen to use an electronic version. In medium- and light-duty applications, the transmission is more than capable to handle modest power in smooth applications, even for the highly discerning Bentley, Jaguar, and Aston Martin crowd.

Identification Tag Decoding

Now that you have found a suitable donor for a rebuild, finding out what you have is just the start. Thankfully, the decoder tag is easy to read. It is located on the passenger's side, rear-most section for later models and middle of the transmission body for earlier models.

The total width of the transmission is 25.750 inches without a tailshaft and will vary based on which vehicle provided the donor.

This tag provides a decent rundown of the transmission. The four-digit code means that this is a 2007 model, and the "P" means that it's a 4L80E. "BS" represents the model, and the upper-right number states the transmission's assembly-as-shipped number.

Here is another identification tag located slightly behind the previous tag on the passenger's side. The model shows "BS," and "P" is a for Hydra-matic 4L80E or 4L80EHD. The model year is stamped as "07" (meaning 2007), and the "6" shows the calendar year, which is followed by the Julian calendar date (the 235th day).

The two tags are shown in relation to one another.

The most important informa-tion that this tag will provide is the year, from which you can determine whether the transmission is a good version or an older, less-desirable ver-sion. The differences in models will be spelled out later.

Once the identification tag has been located, the numbers are as follows:

1. The model year of the vehicle (i.e., 99 is 1999, 04 is 2004, etc.)
2. The calendar year in which the transmission was built. This number can be different than the model year, as build dates for each are not concurrent.
3. This three-digit number is the Julian Date. This is the day of the year (out of 365) that it was built. For example, ours reads "235," which is August 23.
4. This should say "P," as it desig-nates this transmission as the 4L80E model. If you see a "D," it is the 4L60E.
5. This is the transmission model.

There may also be a sticker just forward of the metal identification tag that will provide essentially the same information but may add the loca-tion where it was manufactured. All 4L80Es were built in Ypsilanti Town-ship in Michigan at the Willow Run Transmission factory, which was also called Ypsilanti Transmission Opera-tions (YTO). B-24 bombers were built at this site in 1941, but it is currently closed and is pending sale or demoli-tion at the time of this writing.

Mating Old and New

It's tempting to combine an older transmission with a newer-technology engine. The bene-fits are certainly there when it comes to making the marriage happen. The process is fairly simple with the right combination of parts. The main rea-son why these replacement parts are needed is because the LS-style crank-shaft is shorter than the crankshaft that was used during the small-block Chevy/big-block Chevy era of engines that dominated the market for the better part of 40 years.

To complete the mating, a fly-wheel and a spacer are needed from a 3/4-ton GM truck or any of the vehi-cles listed previously. If you don't want to waste your time in the junk-yard or trying your luck on eBay, use the following GM part numbers to buy a brand new for a fairly inexpen-sive price.

Another option is to order a torque converter that already has the correct offset and correct mounting pads that will bolt up to a 4.8-liter LS motor or 5.3-liter LS flexplate.

Mating New to Old

While Henry Ford never intended for his cars to be stuffed with small-block Chevy motors, that didn't stop anyone from doing so. And while he may forever spin in his grave over this com-plete and utter travesty, having a carbureted-controlled, old-school engine paired to the smooth-shifting, computer-controlled transmission is probably on a few to-do lists.

To accomplish this, bypass the 12 o'clock bolt bellhousing hole because the older small-block engines didn't have them available. The torque con-verter on the stock 4L80E will have six bolt locations, but older-style small-block engines only came with three-bolt hole styles. The three bolts will line up but not all six.

For the cooling lines, find a way to splice the 4L80E's 3/8-inch cool-ing lines to the older style TH400's 5/16-inch lines. This is assuming that you are using an older-style radiator with built-in transmission cooling. This could be done using 1/4-inch national pipe straight mechanical (NPSM) adapters to 5/16-inch lines.

A 4L80E slip yoke is required to be mated to the now-shortened drivesh-aft because it is longer than a TH400, so that completes the physical modifi-cations that need to be made.

Finally, the electronics need a method for control. There are many aftermarket options available, includ-ing the Compushift Sport or Pro models, which are built in the United States and touted to be "plug and play."

The benefit of using a computer-controlled transmission over an old-school style is fairly impressive. Not only does it provide the added benefit of an overdrive gear in an old-school hot rod but it also gives the ability to change shift points and firmness on the fly with the Bluetooth support. This support is now common on many applications with several preset combinations built in. This also means that the option to add a unique paddle-shift option is available.

Key Part Numbers	
Part	Part Number
Flywheel	19260102
Spacer	12563532
Bolts (6)	19257940

DISASSEMBLY

You've taken the first step toward becoming a wizard in the mysterious art of fluid dynamics that is the automatic transmission. This chapter will be a pictorial guide and reference for that inevitable time when you walk away from the project, move parts around, and forget the order in which things go back together, even though you told yourself that you could remember such things.

The good news is that disassembly is the easiest part of the process. It should take 20 to 30 minutes, even if you've never performed the procedure before. You will need some basic hand tools to complete the teardown.

Keep the book open during the assembly phase, as we had to reference teardown photos to make sure that all of the correct bolts and parts were reassembled in the same order. Take notes as well to remind yourself where things go.

Work Area

The first and most important item that is required is a work area that is large enough and clean. As the parts are being removed, have a large, clean area to organize the parts. Laying parts end to end will help you reassemble the 4L80E more easily and reduce confusion. We recommend having a sizable clean table (preferably metal so that it's easy to clean) and a separate area to tear down your 4L80E.

Even with a perfectly good rebuildable core from a junkyard, friend, or your own truck, rebuilding the 4L80E transmission will be a giant mess of parts and fluid no matter how careful you are. You've been warned.

Prior to removing anything, we recommend placing a large tray with a decent lip on the edge, such as a large industrial baking pan, under the transmission to catch all the fluid that is bound to come dribbling out with no end in sight. It frankly does not matter how well the oil was drained out of the case, there will always be at minimum 1 to 2 quarts of transmission fluid still skulking around inside. Just like any fluid,

This is the entirety of the 4L80E's guts in the order in which they were removed. When it comes time to reassemble it, do one section at a time. The entire build can be intimidating if it is your first time. However, it isn't absolutely necessary to understand how it all works to get it to work properly.

it will find the lowest point it can reach and just sit, waiting for it to be given an opportunity to flow downward. Believe it or not, the 4L80E is designed to keep as much fluid inside the case as possible, so be prepared to dump fluid into the pan.

Wear dirty clothes and have a couple rolls of thick shop towels ready. They will come in handy when there is a spill or you inevitably get your hands dirty and need to rub your eyes.

Safety

This should go without saying, but it's necessary to reiterate for those who have a strong desire to taste transmission fluid: don't do it.

While ingesting used or new transmission fluid may not be ultimately as harmful as coolant or brake fluid, it can induce vomiting and cause an upset stomach. Used transmission fluid is a concern because it may contain microscopic metal pieces.

Also, if used or new transmission fluid gets in your eyes, the poison control center recommends flushing your eyes thoroughly and seeking medical attention. For any concern with fluid contact, seek immediate medical attention. ∎

Tools and Supplies

The teardown of most transmissions is fairly straightforward and easy. The 4L80E is no different, and the tools that are required are owned by even the most novice of car folk.

The teardown process can be very educational on many fronts. It will provide a reasonably good education regarding how everything is disassembled and assembled. Next, it can provide a great deal of information about how your 4L80E has been treated over time. Finally, tearing into the 4L80E case can remove much of the mystery that surrounds the enigmatic automatic transmission.

These are the tools that are needed to take apart the 4L80E. The only specialty tool that may be needed is a set of snap-ring pliers. These can be found at virtually any auto parts retail store.

From the outside, it can be a confusing web of tubes, pipes, clutches, and fluid passages. As each part is removed in its specific order, it will reveal the deliberate precision that allows these engineering feats to function.

Once a decent work station and oil catch pan are ready, the following tools will be needed to tear down any 4L80E. The good news here is that only one special tool will be needed, and it can be found at any automotive store, hardware store, discount tool store, or big box home repair store. The tools needed are:

• A long, flat-blade standard screwdriver. You'll use it to pry and move large snap rings in and out of place. This is the best tool to remove those rings and reach deep places inside the case.
• A 15-mm open-ended wrench. A few places, such as the shifter shaft, require the use of an open-ended wrench.
• A medium-size adjustable wrench. A regular, appropriately sized wrench works just as well, but there are a few places where, despite the fasteners being metric, it makes sense to use an adjustable wrench for quick tweaking.

• 8-mm, 10-mm, 13-mm, and 3/8-inch sockets. These can all be regular sized or deep well (both work well).
• A deep-well 10-mm socket will be used to reach a couple buried bolts.
• A 5/32-inch hex key socket or Allen wrench. This unique socket is required on only one bolt that holds a specific part of the valve body to the case.
• A pair of snap-ring pliers. There are a few instances where the two-pronged version is needed to get into tight spaces. This is the only "special" tool that will be needed, but cheap versions are readily available from the usual places.
• A small screwdriver or pick. The 4L80E has a few smaller pieces that need a pick to pull out or manipulate.
• A long-reach, angled pair of needle-nose pliers. The 4L80E case can be quite cavernous at times, so it helps to have a little bit extra reach in a few places.

With all things considered, this is a short list. Gathering tools will be the easiest part of the build, so enjoy the little break before the work begins.

A standard 4L80E rebuild kit contains the following parts: clutch packs, clutch steels, a number of gaskets, seals, and a new transmission filter.

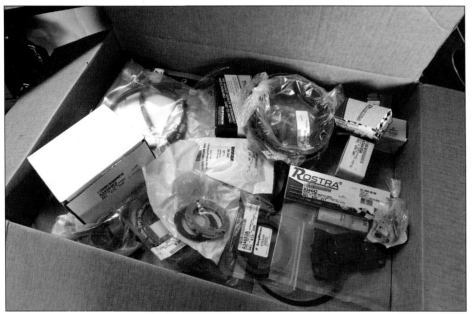

In our Monster Transmission box, we not only received the usual rebuild supplies but we also a number of roller bearings and beefed-up parts, including new solenoids.

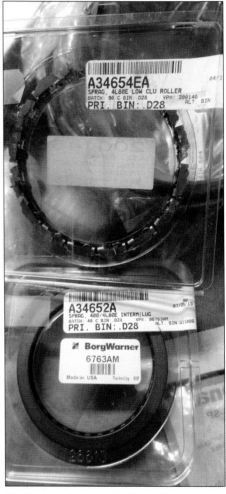

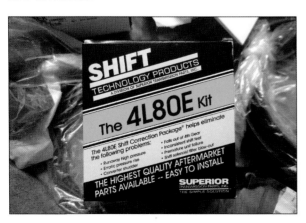

The kit also comes with a shift kit that promises a number of things, including better-feeling shifts, elimination of premature unit failure, and prolonged transmission life.

Roller bearings are a key when passing any decent amount of power through a 4L80E transmission. These came in the Monster Transmission kit that we received.

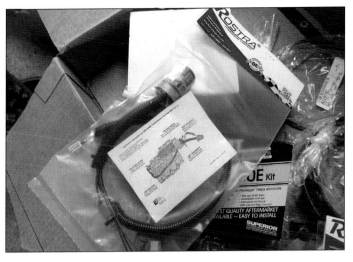

A new wiring harness is typical in any rebuild kit, and our kit was no different. The new harness will be fairly firm and may need some wrangling to get it into place during final assembly.

Cleaning

I was taught at a very early age that cleaning before beginning tear-down makes life a million times easier in the long run, so a little elbow grease before even turning a wrench will pay off. When pressure washing, it is impossible to keep water or oil from entering or escaping the 4L80E case. So, just accept that as a fact of life. The oil-cooler lines, dipstick-tube opening, and all of the seals are potential locations for such occurrences.

Before turning a wrench, find a decently powerful power sprayer, a few cans of degreaser, and a stiff bristle brush. Let the power washer warm up while dousing the case with degreaser (I prefer orange scent because that's how a 4L80E should smell) and aggressively attacking all nooks and crannies of the case with the brush.

Remove the grime using the power sprayer until you are satisfied that the case is clean. We will be doing this again when the case is empty, and we can degrease and use the appropriate solvent to clean the interior. By cleaning the outside at this point, the chances of contaminating your work with outside grime are lowered.

We scored two versions of the 4L80E from Sharadon Performance, a local speed shop. This is typically how you will find them: dirty, a little rusty, and usually missing the tailshaft.

Step one is to spray down the outer case with degreaser. A full can is usually a good start. Scrubbing the outer case will help loosen the grime. Many of these carcasses will have hundreds of thousands of miles on them.

Do not allow transmission fluid to run down sewer drains. It can contaminate ground or drinking water. Also, do not take a dirty case to a car wash that has power washers. Many car-wash facilities recycle the water, and the addition of transmission fluid to the water creates an additional cleaning cost for the car-wash owner. The best plan is to take the case and usable components to a transmission shop, where they can be placed in the hot-tank parts cleaner.

It is recommended to wear the appropriate personal protective equipment (PPE), such as eyewear and protective gloves. Gloves are nice but may get snagged and torn on a sharp part and cause bloodshed, which negates their benefits. If you are careful, wearing tight-fitting nitrile gloves can be very useful to keep clean.

Disassembly

As you tear down the 4L80E, wash the parts in a solvent-based parts washer or in a plastic bin that is safe for fluids, such as mineral spirits, that can be used to brush and clean parts. As each part is removed, clean it and put it in the order on your bench. This will keep the parts organized and tidy.

Many types of solvents are available, such as mineral spirits, turpentine, d-limonene, and the tried-and-true Simple Green. Always clean in a well-ventilated area to avoid overexposure to chemical fumes.

Petroleum-based solvents work as well, such as kerosene or diesel fuel, but they often can be messy and leave a bad odor for long periods of time. In addition, brake cleaner is a cheap option to use as an automotive degreaser.

The fully dry case weighs 236 pounds and can weigh as much as 260 pounds when it is full of fluid. While I was able to get the transmission up on my bench by myself, it's recommended to get help and lift with the legs to save your back.

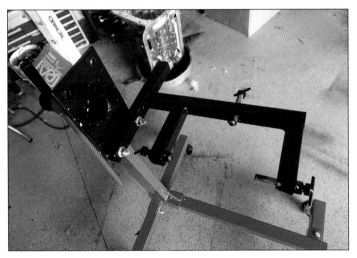

This engine stand adapter isn't necessary to rebuild a transmission, but it certainly makes the job a lot easier. This adapter is different than the one used for the TH400 (even though they are related), so purchase the 4L80E version.

Engine Stand Fixture

After way too long, I decided to break down and buy a dedicated fixture to hold my 4L80E. I found a decent version on eBay that cost about $150 (shipping included), and while I do not perform this work full time, I found the investment to be worth the money.

Sure, the transmission could be disassembled on the bench (as I did before I wised up) and then

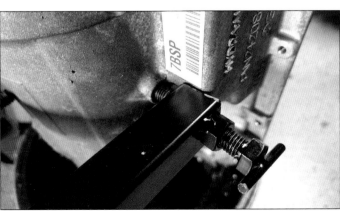

The dedicated stand we purchased allowed us to use this casting mold hole to mount our unit to our engine stand.

The advantage to purchasing this stand is that it adapts directly to any engine stand and allows the 4L80E to be rotated into virtually any position. There will be prolonged times when the underside will be worked on. You can also build an adapter with some steel tube and welded-on nuts if you prefer not to buy one.

later put back together with a poor, overworked 5-gallon bucket. However, the ability to rotate and position the case has saved me a lot of time.

There are a few tricky angles that require the case to be held very still to align a part or maneuver, for example, a snap ring into place. The version that I found allowed me to bolt the case to the fixture and then attach it to any standard engine stand. This provided several clocked positions to lock my 4L80E in place, as that was a feature of the stand. The fixture is specific to the 4L80E due to its larger-than-usual case body. So, any standard GM transmission stand will not work with an adapter or this specific type of stand.

Oil Pan Removal

After the outside of the transmission case is clean, start by removing the oil pan from the underside of the case with a 10-mm socket. Since I wasn't concerned with stripping a bolt, I reached for my impact socket gun and removed one full side of bolts. Then, I turned the case on its side, which allowed any fluid that found its way into the pan to escape in a controlled manner. If I had the stand ready, I could have controlled the spillage more easily.

Removing the Oil Pan

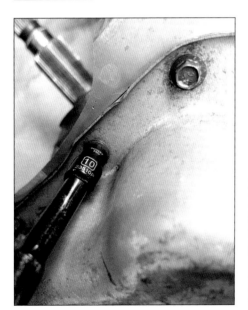

1 *Disassembly requires a 10-mm socket in various places, and this is no different. Zipping them off with a mini-impact gets the work done quickly.*

2 *Grab some paper towels because there is bound to be at least a quart of residual fluid left in the transmission filter, oil passageways, and case. While most of it resides in the torque converter, much of it stays well hidden. We recommend using gloves and a large pan to keep the mess to a minimum.*

3 We were fairly lucky to see that our rebuild core did not have a lot of shiny metal flakes nor did it have any shards of metal stuck to the pan magnet. All the fluid appeared to be clean with no obvious internal damage.

4 The underside of our donor 4L80E looks pretty good and does not have any obvious damage or wear. The fluid also looked promising.

Once the fluid stops flowing, remove the remaining bolts to reveal the bottom half of the transmission. Now, inspect the drain bolt, which is magnetic and attracts any metal shavings. Finding a lack of material buildup is a good sign, but it is not definitive that the transmission is in good condition. Remember that the absence of evidence of abuse is not evidence of absence of abuse.

Oil Filter

Thankfully, our version is in good fluid order and didn't show any of the telltale signs of abuse—at least not from this inspection.

Next, the oil filter is removed with a firm tug and a twist, as it is held in with just pressure. In our version, there was still quite a lot of fluid residing in the filter. Get used to being wet and dirty through the rest of the process.

The transmission filter will have quite a bit of fluid still inside. It pulls off with a gentle tug away from the case. It should be a snug fit.

The large, round bulb at the bottom is called the rear servo cover. This is spring-loaded, so take care when removing this cover, as it may still be under some pressure. The main wiring harness is also visible as it exits out the side of the case. Take note of the orientation of items such as the crossover tube to increase efficiency when it's time to reassemble.

Once the wiring harness and filter are removed, take note of the bolts (shown here) on the valve body itself. Different lengths are specific to each bolt hole. There are two main sizes, and it will not go back together properly if these are mixed up. Our rebuildable core came with a TransGo shift kit of which we were not previously aware. This is evident by the brass pressure plate on the lower left.

Valve Body and Wiring Harness

A visual inspection of the valve body and wiring harness indicated that our version was acceptable to be a donor. From here, teardown can begin in any number of places. We started with the wiring harness and external connector. With this out of the way, we have access to the rest of the vital components.

The transmission oil filter is only held in with pressure. A quick yank can remove it.

This is what it looks like without the filter in place; everything is tight and packed into place. When reassembling the pan, everything must be in its exact place. Otherwise, the pan will not fit correctly. Do not force things back together. Everything will drop into place neatly when it is aligned properly.

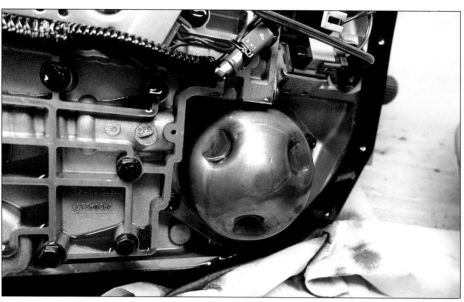

The rear servo holds several parts that must be kept in order. Document all of the parts and make sure that they stay in order for reassembly.

The spring detent for the shifter assembly provides a positive click *when the shifter is engaged, gear to gear. The shifter shaft exits the driver's side and operates the reverse linkage and all forward gears with the pin seen at the bottom of the shaft.*

Crossover Tube

The crossover tube is next item to be removed to be cleaned and set aside. Note that the early 1991–1996 cases have a much larger tube due to their rear-lubrication style of oil disbursement.

Based on the identification tag, our 4L80E came out of a 2007 4WD vehicle (most likely a truck). Our late-model version, marked in history as being from 1997 and newer, has center lubrication, meaning that the oil is disbursed from the center of the case rather than from the rear. This was a much-needed improvement from previous models, as it helped to spread oil to critical parts more evenly and reduce overheating issues.

Manual Detent Assembly

The next item on the list is the manual detent assembly. This consists of two 10-mm bolts and a small piece of spring metal. This provides positive feedback to the driver, who is moving gears. It also ensures that the shift valve is in the correct station every single time so that the fluid goes exactly where its means to.

Removing the Wiring Harness

1 *The wiring harness can be removed with a small, flat-blade screwdriver. It is pushed backward into the case for removal.*

2 *Removing the clips is simple and easy because they have been soaking in oil for their entire lives. There should be no rusty parts or frozen, brittle clips. What a joy!*

3 The wiring harness exterior connector is only held in with pressure from the clips and an O-ring. It's not uncommon for these rings to fail and cause a leak.

4 This crossover tube is retained by one hold-down clamp that is bolted through the valve body itself. Once the tube is free, remove it by gently pulling backward. Note the black and grey solenoids: the upper black solenoid is referred to as "A," and the grey lower one is referred to as "B."

5 The wiring harness has been completely removed. Moving counterclockwise, starting at the left-most clip, they attach to the force motor. The clip at the 7 o'clock position attaches to the pulse width modulation (PWM) solenoid. This solenoid sends the torque converter a pulse signal for when to go in and out of lockup mode. The bright red clip at the 5 o'clock position attaches to the PSM board on the valve body, the cream-colored clip goes to solenoid A, and the darker grey one leads to solenoid B with the red-green wires. The zip-tied plastic piece is the temperature sensor, which may be different on older models that may have a third wire and clip near the PWM side.

Valve Body Removal

We can now move on to the valve body. Remove the valve body with the transmission upside down or at least leaning away from the oil pan. Using a 10-mm socket, lightly loosen all of the bolts that can be seen. The valve body will be full of transmission fluid, so have a drip pan ready.

Carefully loosen all of the bolts before attempting removal. Once it is loose, the valve body should come right off of the 4L80E case without much effort. Do not force the valve body or attempt to pry at it because doing so will damage the unit.

Once all of the bolts are loose, switch to an 8-mm socket and loosen

and remove the six pressure switch manifold (PSM) bolts. Set these bolts aside and label them appropriately. They can be reused.

Your valve body is now ready to be removed. Pull up gently but firmly to separate the valve body from the case. This will normally bring with it the spacer plate and both gaskets.

Removing the Valve Body

1 The valve body is attached by a seemingly endless number of 10-mm head bolts. These will be reused, so make sure to keep them in order from which they came.

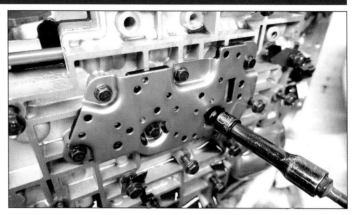

2 The pressure switch manifold (PSM) is attached with 8-mm bolts, so it is fairly easy to make sure which bolts go here in the end. The PSM's job is to tell the computer where the shifter selector lever is (i.e., Park, Neutral, Drive, etc.).

3 The underside of the valve body has a metal spacer plate and two gaskets; they are not identical and will require notice of the correct order and orientation. It will be fairly obvious where it goes when you go back to put it all together. This is not the original valve body plate and is most likely a Trans-go shift kit. We can identify this using the thickness of the plate, which is almost triple the stock size.

Next, move the valve body to the parts cleaner.

Check Balls

With the valve body removed, a series of check balls will be found in the oil pressure passages. There should be eight total check balls, and each ball is 0.250 inch. If the transmission is not facing the correct orientation, these little balls can fall out and scatter on the floor. When performing this step with the transmission still in the car, collecting these check balls is not an issue with the help of a shop magnet. However, replacing them can be tricky.

Removing Check Balls

1 With the case tilted back slightly when the valve body was removed, cradle the check balls in the original positions and make note of them for future reference. There are eight total check balls in a stock rebuild. Shift kits will often remove one or more check balls.

2 The easy way to remove the check balls and not lose them is to use a light magnet to capture them.

3 The valve body is arguably the most important piece to the transmission. It is often the weak link when big power is put through these transmissions, and it is fiddled with constantly by shift kits and builders. Think of it as the fluid-dynamic brain of the entire unit.

4 Here is the case without the valve body attached. It is a complicated piece of machinery. Keep in mind, with modern casting and machining processes having such tight tolerances, the edges are very sharp, and often blood and transmission fluid look very similar. The check ball locations are shown here for reference. Ours came with a shift kit that removed the lower left-most ball and left the remaining balls intact. There should be eight total balls, but we only had seven.

Parking Lock Bracket

Another small part that comes out is the parking lock bracket, which is attached with a 13-mm bolt. The bracket is connected to a long shaft that is connected to the shifter shaft. This bracket holds the shaft in place to engage the parking brake pawl when the driver moves the selector stalk to the "P" position.

Parking Lock Actuator Shaft

From there, the parking lock actuator connects to the manual

If you wish to remove the parking pawl, there is a small retainer clip that holds the pin in place and a plug on the back side that will need to be removed. Removing the pawl is not necessary for basic- and moderate-level rebuilds.

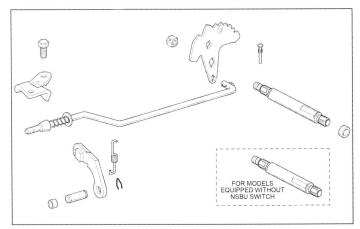

This is a simplified view of the parking lock and actuator assembly. (Image Courtesy General Motors)

Before removing the parking lock bracket, note the orientation of the parking-brake return spring on the parking lock pawl.

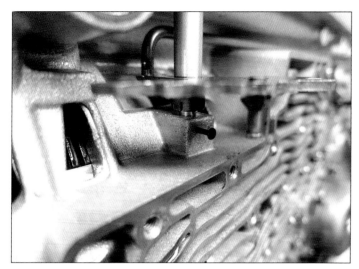

The shifter shaft pin looks like a small nail with grooves cut in the side to dig into the aluminum case. It is held in place by this pin. A quick tug with a pair of pliers will pull it out cleanly. Keep this in a plastic bag so that you don't lose it; it becomes handy during reassembly. Do not over-drive this pin or break it off in the case because there is no way to retrieve it if it's broken.

shift shaft via the detent lever, which controls the main valve of the 4L80E. To remove the parking lock actuator shaft, remove the manual shift shaft and detent plate.

There is a small nail-like pin that holds the manual shift shaft in place. Use a pair of needle-nose pliers to remove this pin, as it is only held in with pressure. Notice that this pin has grooves in its sides to hold it into the case. This is a unique piece and should not be lost.

Detent Plate Removal

To remove the manual detent plate, use a 15-mm open-ended wrench and an adjustable crescent wrench on the outside of the manual-shift shaft. Loosen the nut on the inside and remove it. The shaft should slide out easily from the case, freeing the detent plate and the parking shaft.

Take note of the orientation of not only the detent plate but also the parking lock shaft because it can only be installed one way. This was discovered the hard way during our rebuild process.

Removing the Shift Level Arm and Associated Parts

1 *The detent spring comes out by removing two 10-mm bolts. Keep these labeled and together for reassembly.*

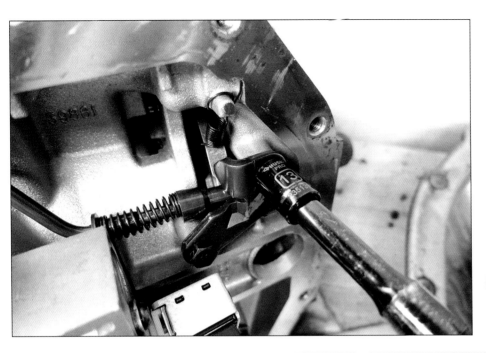

2 The parking lock bracket is attached with two 13-mm bolts, which are also holding the parking position actuator assembly in place.

3 With the nail removed, use a 15-mm wrench to remove the nut while holding the shifter pin steady.

4 Now, the shifter pin can easily be removed, and the shifter level and pin assembly will come out as well.

The bottom side of the case contains a few more parts that need to be removed and reconditioned. The rear servo cover comes off with six 10-mm bolts. This may be under a bit of pressure from the springs inside, so take caution when removing the bolts.

Inside the rear servo cover is a metal gasket, a retaining clip, the servo piston, and an oil seal. Under the piston are two springs (one inside another): the rear piston accumulator and the rear band applicator. The assembly actuates the reverse gear and rear band assembly.

Directly near the big round rear servo cover lies the front servo piston, spring, another piston underneath that, and a small spring. These are held in with pressure and can be pulled out easily with your hands.

Removing the Rear Servo and Piston

1 The rear servo cover can be removed with six 10-mm bolts. They should be lightly torqued; so, they won't need a lot of force.

2 Many rebuild kits supply this metal gasket.

3 A small C-clip holds the spring and rear band applicator shaft in place. Keep and retain this clip, as it will be needed for reassembly.

4 Once the C-clip is removed, several parts will be found inside the cup, including a few springs, gaskets, and seals.

5 The low and reverse servo cover comes out by removing six bolts and is under spring pressure.

6 Inside the cap is the servo piston, a gasket, and an O-ring.

7 Left inside the block shown here are the piston pin, springs, and retainers.

Internal Bolts

Two bolts must be removed so that the innards of the 4L80E can be removed.

One is located just above the rear servo cover and is buried flush with the oil passages under the valve body. This is a 3/8-inch, 12-point bolt and is designed to locate and lock the center support in place. GM recommends to replace this bolt. When it comes time to replace it, torque it to 32 ft-lbs.

The second bolt is also buried quite deep in the case and requires a 5/32-inch Allen key socket or a 40 torx bit. It is the bolt that holds the fourth gear (overdrive) clutch housing in place. GM recommends to replace this bolt as well. When it is replaced, torque it to 17 ft-lbs.

This bolt is a great method of determining if a build is going smoothly or not. If this bolt does not line up perfectly with the overdrive clutch housing, then there are poten-tial misalignment issues somewhere below. If all is aligned well, then proceed to completing the build.

Once everything from the underside of the transmission is removed and cataloged, move to the front of the 4L80E and address the guts of the beast.

Front Oil Pump

The front oil pump is attached to the case with seven bolts that come off with a 13-mm regular or deep-well socket. With the bolts removed, the oil pump should slide out gracefully. It will be fairly bulky and heavy, so watch your fingers as you pull it out. There is an official removal tool for this, part number J-38789, which can be purchased for $260 at the time of writing. Otherwise, you can simply pull it out with your hands for free, which is what we did.

The pump should come out nicely and easily, but for the vast majority of 4L80Es, this simply will not happen. As Lonnie Diers of Extreme Automatics said, "Most of these units [that] I see coming in have well over 200,000 miles on them and sometimes over 300,000."

After that many miles, the oil pump can become self-glued to the case. There is a simple workaround for this.

Our pump was being difficult, so we shoved a long-handled screwdriver through the existing hole in the case under the oil pan and pump. This provided some room to place pressure on the back side of the pump and give a few solid raps with a mallet. In most cases, a few hits around the bellhousing will loosen the bond that may have formed over the years and persuade the pump to come out on its own terms.

Do not force the pry bar or screwdriver in the case because we do not want to damage the case. Just apply constant pressure from the back side and provide a few hits to get it to let go.

Removing the Front Oil Pump

1 *The front pump is attached with a series of 13-mm bolts. These are in fairly snug and torqued down, so prepare to give it some considerable force or use an impact gun to remove them.*

2 *A small trick for removing the front pump from the case if it is stuck is to shove a long-handled, flat-blade screwdriver through the hole (shown here). Push the pump forward with medium pressure and hit the side of the case with a dead-blow hammer or rubber mallet so that the bellhousing is not damaged. Tap around the edge of the entire bellhousing, and it should come loose fairly quickly with no drama.*

3 *Other manuals will say to use a special tool or puller to remove the front pump, but that is simply not necessary. The front pump is heavy and contains many parts. Be sure to use two hands, and carefully remove it without nicking the soft aluminum case.*

From there, the oil pump will come out as one unit with the over-run clutch assembly. They can be taken out separately if the O-ring is removed from the turbine shaft (also called the input shaft). Either way works well. However, in our experience, it is not possible to separate the pump from the over-run clutch housing without removing that teeny O-ring. It is that formidable.

Removing the Fourth Gear Clutch

1 *On the outer edge is the fourth clutch backing plate. It is held stationary by a large locating pin on the left.*

2 *This assembly is held in with a large snap ring that can be removed by using a flat-blade screwdriver if you don't have the correct and very expensive snap ring removal tool. We used a screwdriver.*

Next, the fourth clutch housing and clutches, also called the over-drive clutch housing (fourth gear is overdrive), will slide out without much fuss. Just remember to remove the overdrive clutch retaining bolt from the underside of the case.

The clutches can be removed separately from the housing with the removal of a large snap ring, as we did, or as one section. The fourth gear clutch retainer plate may need a bit of attitude adjustment; just note the order in which the plates and clutches are arranged.

Our assembly looked like this when it was removed from the case. Read the clutch discs and steels to get a better idea of how this transmission was treated over its lifetime and to estimate its potential age in miles. While we saw a few burnt spots on the steels, the clutches appeared to have moderate life left in them and did not suffer from too much abuse. These replacements will come in your rebuild kit.

The rear output shaft seal is held in with a snap ring and requires a pair of inner-shaped snap-ring pliers. The best part of the teardown is that it doesn't require any special tools beyond these pliers, which can be found at any generic parts store.

A snap-ring pliers is needed. However, snap rings rarely go bad, so most kits will not have replacements.

The fourth clutch case bolt is a 5/32 Allen key bolt that holds the fourth gear clutch stationary.

This is the front servo piston pin and piston. Inside is a seal and a spring.

The servo piston pin and piston come out without a bolt and are removed just by pulling slightly. Gunk buildup in this area is not uncommon. Replace these O-ring oil seals regardless.

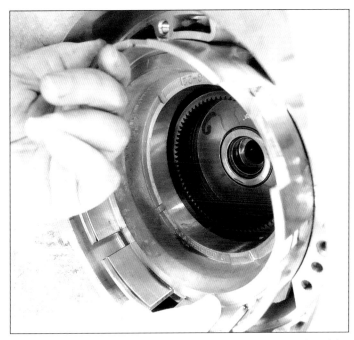

Remove the fourth clutch-case bolt (as shown previously) to remove this large aluminum part that is called the fourth clutch housing. It will slide out when that bolt is removed.

The spring on the back of the fourth clutch housing allows for a smooth transition out of or into fourth gear as pressure increases or decreases. A plugged "fourth apply" passage, damage to the clutch plates, the return-spring assembly, or the piston seals can cause no fourth gear and/or slips in fourth gear.

Forward Clutch Housing Assembly

With the overdrive clutch housing out of the way, another solid and heavy-geared unit can be pulled out: the forward clutch housing assembly. There is yet another special tool for this: a center-support removal tool (part number J-38868). Otherwise, simply reach in and grab it with your hands. Our unit came with helical-cut gears, which means that it was not a heavy-duty unit. It is still usable, but it is just not as desirable as the straight-cut version.

The shaft is retained by this snap ring. The disassembly and reassembly of the 4L80E won't require many special tools, but a pair of snap-ring pliers is a must.

This is the case's center support bolt. It is a 12-point, 3/8-inch bolt. It will need to be removed for complete disassembly.

Parts Inspection

During our teardown, we used the time to inspect parts as they came out of the 4L80E case. We found a few instances where heat had built up and discolored several pieces. This was evidence that this unit had seen a hard life either by towing, plowing, racing, or neglect. It prompted us to look a little more closely than we normally would.

The 4L80E is very sensitive to things such as low lubrication and heat. It is highly recommended to check the fluid level regularly and install a temperature gauge if you do not have one already. Running a 4L80E low on fluid or overheating it even one time can spell certain death. The common myth is that the 4L80E is fragile due to these two factors, but the evidence provides a very different picture. Most reputable shops state that the most common rebuild they do is with 200,000- to 300,000-mile units that have simply been worn out and need new clutch packs. ■

Removing the Direct Clutch Housing Assembly

1 *This is the forward clutch assembly, and it just pulls straight out. If it is inoperable, the forward clutch can cause forward motion in neutral, loss of drive, and harsh shifts from drive to reverse.*

The forward clutch assembly houses many parts and may need to be disassembled if the forward gears are inoperable.

This is the back side of the forward clutch assembly.

2 Note the large snap ring that holds the two halves together. The back part is called the direct clutch drive. The snap ring will can be removed by using with a small flat-blade screwdriver.

4 Underneath the direct clutch hub is a small plastic shim to prevent direct metal-to-metal contact. This is generally replaced when doing a rebuild. However, in a pinch, it can be reused.

3 The blackening that is seen here is heat treating by the factory (not a sign of abuse). The factory will heat treat only this part.

The next item to remove is the direct clutch housing. A C-shaped puller can be used to remove it, but it should come out easily by gripping the middle section.

Inside the direct clutch housing is a set of clutches that is attached with this snap ring. A simple, flat-blade screwdriver should be able to pry it loose.

The front band assembly is pressure fit and has a locating tab (lower part of image).

The next item to be removed is the direct clutch housing assembly. There is yet another specialized tool that can be obtained (part number J-38733). However, the direct clutch housing assembly can also removed by grabbing it with your hands or using two J-shaped hooks to grab the center section and pull up to remove it from the case.

Next, with this assembly, remove the front band assembly, which is indexed by the case and will need prying from a pry bar or larger screwdriver. Some rebuild kits come with new bands, so just make sure to note the orientation of the band for reassembly.

Intermediate Clutch Assembly

Once the band is taken out, the intermediate clutch assembly is ready to be removed. This is held in place by the case and a large snap ring. At this point, you will have a decent set of snap rings, and they should be marked and labeled for the reassembly process because many snap rings in the case look similar in size and shape.

There is a definitely a right and a wrong way to reinstall the snap rings, so pay attention to orientation for reassembly. Remove this snap ring with a quick twist of a flat-blade screwdriver and release the intermediate clutches.

Removing the Intermediate Clutch Assembly

1 Another large snap ring locks into the tabs in the aluminum case. This holds in the intermediate clutch pack.

2 The inner-tube shaft of the output-shaft carrier assembly can be removed with little effort. Note the orientation because this connects to the main shaft of the transmission to create one long main shaft.

3 The intermediate clutch pack also will tell a story. Ours was fairly worn and probably due for a rebuild. The evidence (a few burnt pieces, worn clutches, and a generic shift kit installed) tells us that our 4L80E had seen a few hard shifts and full-throttle pulls.

4 Yet another snap ring holds the final component in place.

5 *The entire rear geartrain assembly can be removed. This assembly houses 55 separate pieces (once disassembled) when paired with the output carrier assembly.*

6 *The backside shows the planetary gears that encircle the sun gear.*

7 *Peering down the case, the sun gear and first-gear assemblies can be seen.*

8 *The sun gear on the main shaft slides off. Inspect it for broken teeth and replace it if necessary.*

Once the clutches are removed, there is another snap ring that holds a large assembly of pieces that will come out all as one unit. It is heavy. To remove it, use the recommended removal tool (part number J-38868) or reach in and grab it. Some folks choose to unload the transmission on a bench. However, using a stand makes disassembly easier because you are not fighting gravity and can manipulate the case in any direction.

This large assembly of pieces is the rear center support, output-carrier assembly, and output shaft. We previously discussed variation differences between model years, and this section is where many of those differences occur.

Our center support section is from a 2007 model, which means that it will not interchange with any case from 1991 to 1996. This also goes for the sun gear shaft and main shaft. These parts are different from early to late models due to the lubrication systems.

Inspect the parts as they are removed. Our planetary gear carrier looked to be in good shape and

The output carrier assembly has a snap ring on the back side that holds the output shaft that exits the rear of the transmission case.

showed no signs of damage, excessive wear, or heat. This is good because a few prior parts had clear signs of heat damage. The sun gear and sun gear shaft slid out without drama.

Case Backside

Once you've made significant teardown progress, turn your attention to the backside of the case. There is a tailshaft in the 2WD version. However, in the 4WD unit (what we have), there is no tailshaft, and there is instant access to the output shaft and snap ring. This is where snap-ring pliers are needed. Without removing this snap ring, it is not be possible to remove the rear lubrication seal and replace it.

Finally, remove the output carrier assembly that includes the transmission main shaft and the output shaft that exits the transmission. Inside is the rear brake band, which is held in by tension and will come out with a long pry bar and a little finagling. Resting against the back of the case are two (possibly three on some models) thrust washers, both with unique designs.

The two washers shown here are the last pieces to remove and should be the first to install during reassembly. In some versions, there is a third piece (an O-ring) that should be installed first, but it is not included in all versions. The washer with the three outward-most prongs is the one against the case. The washer with the three upward-turned prongs faces inside the case.

The flat thrust washer that has three outward-facing prongs goes against the back of the case, while the thrust washer with the four upturned prongs faces upward through the case from the back. This means that when they are installed, the prongs should face you. Some models will have an O-ring seal, and if you did not remove one during this stage, you don't have one.

Congratulations! You've completed the teardown of your 4L80E and are on your way to glory and fame. Sadly, this is the easiest and shortest part of the build.

The case is now completely empty. Perform a thorough inspection for broken tabs or cracks, and completely clean the inside of the case.

REASSEMBLY

Now that everything has been disassembled, cataloged, and placed in the order in which it will be reinstalled into the case, we can begin the rebuild process. This will require the teardown of individual components to replace seals, clutches, and various other components.

If you've already made it this far, you might as well complete the project and do it right. Many of the tasks that we perform on this rebuild are not necessary for every rebuild, and, in a few instances, they only pertain to higher-load applications. However, this section will go through the basic process of rebuilding a 4L80E. It will also provide insight into other areas that you may wish to address during your build.

Before getting started, you may look at the pile of parts and wish that you had just sent it to the local transmission rebuilder and called it a day. It may look daunting and overwhelming at times. However, if you take each section methodically one at a time, the job can be completed in a much less-stressful fashion than trying to complete the entire task at once.

Here is a suggestion: keep this book open to the disassembly section just as much as the reassembly section. In several instances, we looked back at the tear-down images to determine the orientation of parts and the order in which they were removed. If this is your first rebuild, it's normal to be confused at times; embrace it.

Preparation

First, buy, borrow, or rent a transmission stand. The one we used cost about $150 and mounts directly to any standard engine stand. This mount is instrumental for rotating and moving around the 4L80E case.

Second, go slowly. If you rush, you may install it back into the car or truck only to discover that it needs to be removed again.

Third, have a disposable bucket of Dexron handy and don't be afraid to get wet. Reassembly is messy at times.

Finally, have each part and tool as well as grease and all necessary fluids at hand when you are rebuilding. The process goes more smoothly and less painfully when you have everything that you need and aren't wasting time searching for lost items.

Have a bucket of fresh transmission fluid handy because many parts need to be soaked prior to installation. Remember, there is no good way to prime a transmission, and starting it dry is not good.

This green little O-ring may not look like much, but it will prevent the front pump from coming off the input shaft. Most rebuild kits will come with a replacement.

Here's a long, deep shot of our core. It's clean, inspected, and ready to accept our rebuilt parts.

By this point, the transmission pan magnet has been found. Ours was pretty clean and didn't hold any metal shavings. It was a good sign that we were dealing with a good, rebuildable core.

The engine-stand adapter allows for a full 360-degree rotation, which makes the installation of parts, such as the rear brake band, much easier.

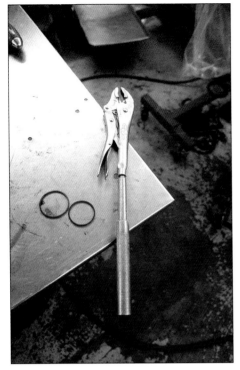

Denny Baierl from Sharadon Performance has this extension on his Vise-Grips, which allows him to use both hands when lowering whole assemblies into place. This will not damage the hardened steel of gears or splined shafts.

Our box of goodies from Monster Transmission was sorted and laid out by part group for less time and frustration. The way it sits here only adds to the confusion.

If you have access to a parts washer, it never hurts to run the valve body through for a thorough cleaning. Despite doing so, we still found grime in many of the tight areas of the valve body.

Rebuild Kit

Before starting the rebuild process, acquire a decent rebuild kit. There are dozens on the market with many various options. Purchase the best rebuild kit that you can afford: buy once, cry once. Our rebuild kit from Monster Transmission (part number MG4L80E-BXSS-04UP) was for 2004-and-newer models. Remember, that 1991–1996 denotes early models and 1996-and-up are late models. Also, there was a small change to the front oil pump's back half in 2004 that differentiates it from all other previous versions.

Our kit came with a standard rebuild kit, clutches, and all of the appropriate seals, but it also came with a box of other parts, includ-ing new solenoids, a shift kit, roller bearings, and modules. This kit is reported to handle much more power: up to 750 hp and 700 ft-lbs of torque. It was chosen so that we can show a basic rebuild and a few upgrades that can be performed with the 4L80E already disassembled.

Once we were squared away with our kit, we organized the parts by laying everything out on a table. Then, Denny Baierl from Sharadon Performance in Hugo, Minnesota, took our 4L80E case and ran it and all of the reusable parts through the parts solvent wash station. The cleaner that everything is prior to rebuilding, the better.

Lonnie Diers at Extreme Automatics told us that every single rebuild that has failed has been due to a dirty work environment and dirty work conditions that contaminated the transmission. He said to keep everything clean throughout the entire process and replace everything that needs replacing, regardless of whether it seemed passable or not.

When putting this back together, we often found ourselves marveling at how much ingenuity and engineering it takes to make something like this function as it does.

At Sharadon Performance in Hugo, Minnesota, we used a wash tank with solvent. This ensured that we removed all of the old fluid and potential metal shavings. In theory, using cleaner and a power sprayer could produce the same results. However, if you have access to a wash tank, use it. A decent parts washer should run a few hundred dollars.

A rear main seal is installed with a seal installation tool. An appropriate-size socket works as well.

Rear Main Seal

The build process begins at the tailshaft. Make sure that the 4L80E is firmly in its fixture (or 5-gallon bucket, if you prefer) and work backward. The rear main seal will be a standard seal that is very common and comes out with a good yank of a pry bar. Be careful not to nick or mar the case.

The seal is reinstalled with the appropriate-size seal installation tool or a large socket with a hammer. Next, the rear brake band is slipped into place. This band needs pressure in a few key areas to get it to snap into place.

Rear Output Shaft Assembly

From there, our attention turns to the rear output-shaft assembly. Our steel table has a few different-size holes in it, which allows the various shafts to pass through the table and give us a stable platform to manipulate and work on the assemblies. We use a pick and a standard flat-blade screwdriver to remove the snap ring that connects both halves.

Inside the output carrier assembly is a large, low-sprag roller bearing. Bearings are wearable parts, and while they are not commonly known to go out frequently, it's good insurance to replace them if a kit comes with one. Ours did, so we swapped it.

Here is another important bit of rebuilding knowledge: lube everything with transmission fluid or Assemblee Goo (where applicable) and then lubricate it again. Engines have ways to prime the oil pump to get oil into important places before the initial startup. However, transmissions do not, and they need fluid added liberally to avoid a dry metal-on-metal first start, which is bad.

In this assembly, there are a series of thrust washers, bearings, and seals. The center support alone has four seals that get snugged down with a worm-gear clamp and doused with Assemblee Goo.

There is a small cup plug in the back of each 4L80E. A rebuild kit will come with either a completely plugged piece or one with a small hole. The version with the small hole is a fluid bleed off for 2WD versions while the plugged cup insert is for 4WD applications.

New (left) and old (right) rear brake band assemblies are next to each other. These are under tension, and after some time, they may lose their pressure. So, it's best to replace it since you've come this far.

The rear brake band can be installed once the intermediate clutch piston with roller bearing has been installed over the sun gear.

Nylon Seals

There are several types of nylon seals in the 4L80E transmission. They must be replaced in every instance because they become hard and brittle, which can lead to a catastrophic failure. These can be a bit tricky to install because they do not like to take shape or return to a specific form. They just deform and stay that way.

Removal is easy with a sharp pick, or more commonly, they just snap out of place because they are weak. There is an official tool (part number J-38735) for seal removal that runs between $250 and $300. With that being said, these can be formed (for free) to accept their shape by putting them in place, surrounding them with an appropriate-size worm-gear clamp, and simply tightening it. Let it sit for a moment or two and then release the worm gear clamp. The nylon seal should relent to its new appearance.

Center Support

The center support must seat properly. This is done by spinning and pressing firmly against the carrier assembly. The center support also needs to be compressed against the spring assembly to install the snap ring. The spring assembly does not need to be rebuilt if it appears to be in good shape with no broken springs and has normal endplay of 0.009 to 0.024 inch.

The center support bolt needs to be aligned with the case. We marked the location with a small X with a marker before lowering it into place. The output shaft assembly with the center support can be a challenge to hold steady while lowering it down carefully into the case. Denny used a clever combination of a large pair of Vise-Grips with an extended handle to grip the geared shaft tightly and control its descent. The geared shaft is made of hardened steel, and we were not concerned with marring it because the pair of Vise-Grips is softer than the shaft.

Rebuilding the Output Carrier Assembly

1 Disconnect the two halves of the drum and the shaft. It is a simple matter of using a large snap ring.

2 The reverse band goes in next. It may take some maneuvering because of the tension that is needed to get it to snap into place.

3 This is the low sprag roller bearing replacement. It slides into the reaction carrier.

4 There are only a few roller bearings in the transmission. It's pretty easy to identify which one goes where by the size and shape.

5 Transmissions don't have the ability to be primed with oil prior to the first start-up, so it's important (and frankly quite messy) to douse every component with new transmission fluid before sending it home.

6 There are a series of oil ring seals that need to be replaced. They will come off fairly easily and are usually brittle from age and heat.

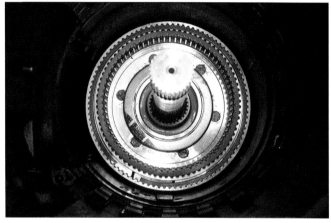

8 Here is an example of an aftermarket close ratio gearset. Notice the number of teeth with straight-cut gears for first gear. Lonnie at Extreme Automatics showed us this comparison to a stock unit.

7 New seals are installed and located in place before cinching them down snug.

Here's an example of an aftermarket 4L80E first gearset.

9 This is a 4L80E aftermarket first gearset that is not installed.

10 This is a factory reaction carrier assembly.

11 Use an aftermarket billet reaction carrier for second gear in a high-performance 4L80E.

12 This factory gearset is machined for a Torrington bearing for a higher-power unit.

The front half of an aftermarket gearset is shown in and out of the case.

gear has a small lip and must face up (toward the front of the case).

Once this is completed, drop everything in and reinstall the snap ring. Be sure to install the beveled snap ring into the case groove with the flat side down (toward the back of the case) and the snap ring opening at the 9 o'clock position with the clock face oriented with the top bellhousing bolt hole at 12 o'clock.

For those wishing to ensure proper end play, set up a dial indicator from the bellhousing to the top of the main shaft. After the snap ring is installed, the acceptable amount of end play is 0.005 to 0.025 inch. There should be a few spacers in the rebuild kit to make up the difference between the output assembly and the rear of the case. This end play check isn't monumentally important to every build, but it is good to know if assemblies are too tight or obviously too loose.

Finally, install the 3/8-inch 12-point center support bolt from the valve-body area and torque it to 32 ft-lbs. Do not overtorque or undertorque this bolt because it is intentionally hollow to allow oil pressure into the intermediate clutch pack.

It may be easier to install this bolt by rotating the 4L80E onto its back and maneuvering the rear output assembly to line up the bolt holes on the center support. If your mount does not rotate like ours, the alternative is to use a small, flat tool to pry the assembly through the direct clutch port in the valve-body portion of the case. It should be along the same axis as the center support bolt. This portion of the rebuild is now complete.

Output Carrier Assembly

The upper half of the output carrier assembly consists of a drum carrier assembly, sun gear, and the sun-gear shaft. Note that the chamfered side of the sun gear faces down (toward the rear of the case) when it is reinstalled. Also, the thrust bearing that goes over the top of the sun

The Center Section Seals

1 The center support and race can now be mated to the output carrier assembly.

2 The new seals are in place. Denny used the worm gear trick to snug these into place and coated them with a liberal amount of Assemblee Goo made by Lubegard.

The support race and assembly can now be placed onto the output carrier shaft assembly.

Before sending the output shaft assembly home, dab it with some assembly grease to keep the thrust washer attached to the output shaft. It's sticky enough to hold the washer and subsequent washer (not shown) in place and will not allow direct metal-to-metal contact.

Our output shaft assembly is ready to be dropped into place. When possible, use the least amount of parts possible to reduce weight and lessen the chance of being nicked or banged up.

Dropping the Center Section into the Case

1 Denny from Sharadon Performance hovers carefully with the entire rear output assembly ready to be dropped in. Everything should fit with very tight tolerances, and no parts should have to be muscled into place. One misaligned component can force you to take the entire thing apart and start anew.

2 After a few attempts at dropping in the rear output assembly, it was decided that a tight pair of Vise-Grips with an extension handle would do less damage.

3 It is easy to miss, but the center support and race assembly are ground in such a way that it will only go in one way. Note the marking and orientation before dropping it into place.

4 Once properly aligned, it will sink into its proper position.

5 Pictured here is the thrust support washer (yellow) around the sun gear and sun gear shaft.

6 *This bolt is what keeps and locates the center support. The assembly is out of line if this bolt does not line up perfectly. Torque this bolt to 32 ft-lbs, but do not overtorque it. The bolt is intentionally designed to be hollow to allow oil to flow to the intermediate clutch pack.*

7 *Next, install the beveled snap ring into the case recesses, making sure the flat side is facing down.*

Intermediate Clutch and Direct Clutch Housing

The next subassembly is the intermediate clutch and direct clutch housing. This involves a series of clutches, clutch steels, a snap ring, and the direct clutch assembly. As with all transmission builds, soaking the parts in transmission fluid prior to assembly is required.

Grab a gallon-sized bucket and fill it with a quart or so of fluid and let the parts marinate for a good moment. The fluid will permeate the surfaces and be ready for the first start-up.

The intermediate clutch starts with clutch discs and plates. First, there is a steel plate that is alternating with

Denny from Sharadon Performance has built countless transmissions to handle high horsepower and strongly emphasized having a bucket of brand-new transmission fluid ready. Since you cannot prime a transmission like an engine, pre-lube and soak internal transmission parts so that you do not have a dry-start condition that risks destroying all of your hard work.

Preparing and Installing the Intermediate Clutch

1 Our clutches receive a nice soaking bath, allowing fluid to completely permeate through the discs.

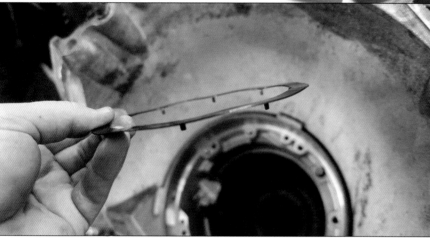

2 These thin shims, often referred to as wave plates or wavy plates, are officially called clutch plates by GM. They are intentionally bent like this.

3 Directly after the rear output assembly is the intermediate clutch pack. Remember, a solid metal plate goes first, and then it alternates with a wearable clutch disc, etc.

4 *Finally, the intermediate clutch is capped by a thicker plate that is called a backer or pressure plate.*

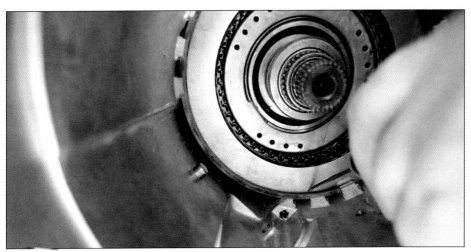

5 *Another snap ring will hold the clutch pack into place. It can be fairly easy to mix up the snap rings, as many are similarly sized.*

a coated clutch disc. This is then topped off with a "wavy" plate, which has some spring to it and appears to be deformed. However, it is intentionally bent to look wavy.

On top of the wavy plate is a clutch backing plate, which is a thicker steel plate meant to sandwich the clutch pack down. This also gets a snap ring that should be left open at the 9 o'clock position (12 o'clock being top center bellhousing bolt).

Check the end play with a feeler gauge between the backing plate and the snap ring. Normal end play movement is between 0.040 and 0.107 inch.

Next, the front band assembly is snapped into place inside the case with the aid of a locating pin that is called a band anchor. After the front band assembly has been installed, install the direct clutch housing. The direct clutch housing houses a clutch pack (five 0.0915-inch steel plates, one wavy plate, and five 0.080-inch clutch discs), one of two sprag assemblies, a series of seals, and a piston.

To remove the piston, a special removal tool (part number J-23327) is needed, which will be used on other assemblies as well. This will compress the spring cage and allow for the removal of the snap ring that holds the pieces in place.

When replacing the piston, make sure to rotate it into position until it's fully seated. Replace the spring cage in reverse order, going slowly and evenly and replacing the snap ring. When the sprag and intermediate clutch race are installed with a snap ring, it should spin freely clockwise with the gears facing up (upside down from installation from the top-down orientation). Piston travel for this operation is valid between 0.121 and 0.236 inch.

Alternate steel rings and friction discs, starting with the wavy plate, then a steel disc, and install all five steel and friction discs. Follow that with the direct clutch backing plate and snap ring. It is now ready to be reinstalled into the case.

Prior to the attempt to send it home, it's imperative to line up the clutches and plates by either lining them up perfectly with a flat object (like a screwdriver) or slowly rotating the direct clutch housing and letting it drop into place once it has engaged that clutch pack. Make sure that it is fully seated before moving on to the next step. Everything should fit in a nice little package once it is fully assembled with no force needed.

The specific installation tool is J-38733, but through various attempts to getting it seat properly, Denny found that the most direct route was to lower it down by the spring cage with two hooked picks. This provided plenty of room for his hands as well as the ability to lower it down gently onto the intermediate clutch pack.

The front band assembly is notched, as shown here. It can only be installed one way and is a very snug fit. Prepare to wrangle and wrestle this piece a bit.

Once it is lowered down, engage all of the clutches and clutch discs until it is fully seated into position. Make sure that the direct clutch housing moves freely. If not, there may be something binding.

Forward Clutch Housing Assembly

Now, our attention shifts to the forward clutch housing and all of its guts. Start by removing the snap ring that holds the direct clutch hub and the forward clutch housing assembly. Underneath is a spring and retainer assembly; an inner, outer, and center clutch seal; and a clutch piston along with a clutch pack and forward clutch hub. Inspect all of the parts, including the springs, for any excessive damage or wear, and then clean them thoroughly.

Removal of the spring assembly is usually not necessary unless it is damaged in some way and needs to be replaced or you wish to replace the forward clutch piston. Compress the springs with a tool, such as a clutch spring compressor (part number J-23327), which costs about $60.

Once compressed, remove the snap ring with a pair of snap-ring pliers and slowly release the tension from the compression tool. Installation of the piston requires a small rotation to get it into position and the reverse order of the compression tool, remembering to replace the bronze thrust washer on the inside of the forward clutch hub. A dab of Assemblee Goo will help keep it in place for reassembly.

When the snap ring is removed, the direct clutch hub and forward clutch hub can be lifted off, revealing the clutch plates and clutch steels. There will be five 0.0775-inch flat steel plates, one dished 0.054-inch plate, and five 0.080-inch clutch coated discs. Alternating clutch steels and clutch discs, align all of the teeth with a small flat-blade screwdriver, drop the forward clutch hub through the splines, and let it completely seat.

This may take a few tries before it seats properly. A solid method for aligning the clutch plates is to rotate the hub slowly and put light pressure in a downward motion to allow the hub to fall into the lugs of the clutch liners. You will know this has worked when the hub drops slightly and all of the discs spin freely with the hub. Get used to this method because it will apply in every clutch replacement situation.

Apply the bronze thrust washer to the top of the forward clutch hub and top the assembly off with the direct clutch driving hub. This part looks like a hat with geared teeth on top.

Finish the assembly rebuild with the correct snap ring that was just removed. To ensure correct piston travel, check it with compressed air. To do this, install the turbine shaft while out of the case and blow air between the two sealing rings. Piston travel for this operation is valid between 0.121 and 0.236 inch.

Once you are satisfied with the forward clutch housing and carrier assembly, align the clutch friction discs and clutch steel discs inside the direct clutch housing. This will allow a smoother drop in of the forward clutch assembly.

If all goes according to plan, it should drop in. However, in the case that it gets hung up, rotate the forward clutch carrier until it fully seats. This procedure of aligning clutches and dropping geared parts between them will be repeated a number of times throughout the build.

Replacing Clutches in the Forward Clutch Assembly

1 The direct clutch drive comes off with the removal of this snap ring (shown here).

2 Once the small hat called the direct clutch drive is taken off, you can remove the forward clutch drive hub (shown on Denny's finger). There is another clutch pack inside the forward clutch housing assembly.

3 Once the clutch pack is removed, it can be replaced with newly fluid soaked discs. We used an analog caliper to determine exactly which clutch pack needed to be used.

4 Using the same logic and method as before, the clutch steels and clutch discs are alternated.

5 On the bottom side of the forward clutch drive hub is a thrust clutch hub house washer.

Adding New Clutches in the Forward Clutch Assembly

2 Denny aligned all of the plates and discs and slid the hub into place. Do not force this into place. A quick way to align them is to drop the hub into place and rotate gently until you feel the hub drop into place. Repeat this rotation until it has bottomed out.

1 Clutches and steels need to be alternated, and the teeth need to be lined up properly so that the carrier assembly can be slid into place.

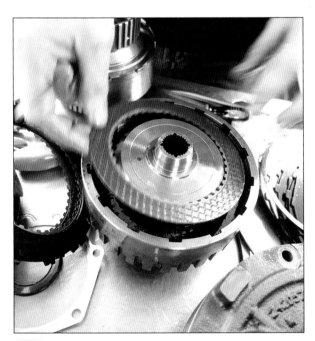

3 Denny suggested dropping the few remaining discs and plates in place rather than having to fight the entire stack at once.

4 The final clutch plate can be put in place.

6 *The final piece is a wavy, dished clutch plate. Some people have chosen to remove these small pieces, but it is recommended to keep them in their original location, not the garbage.*

5 *The final thick clutch plate can be laid into place, awaiting the cover and snap ring.*

7 *A new thrust washer is held in place with assembly lube. This is just sticky enough to hold small parts long enough to install them.*

Dropping this assembly in place can be done with the official tool (part number J-38358-A), which will set you back about $40. It can also be done the normal way by gently lowering it in with your hands and pushing from the inside of the housing assembly to keep it steady and from falling too fast. Do not forget to reinstall the carrier thrust bearing on top before moving on to the overdrive clutch.

8 The forward clutch housing assembly can now be put in place.

9 The forward clutch housing should fit and sit flush with this ridge in the 4L80E case.

Installing the Fourth Gear Clutch Pack

1 The fourth gear clutch pack can now be installed, just like the rest with metal plates separating the clutch discs and the thicker backing plates being the last to be installed.

2 After a few attempts at aligning the discs and plates, we discovered a simple method with a high success rate. We used a long, thin, flat-blade screwdriver to manually align the plates and carefully dropped whatever appropriate piece into plate without rotating it.

3 *Here are properly aligned clutch discs and plates.*

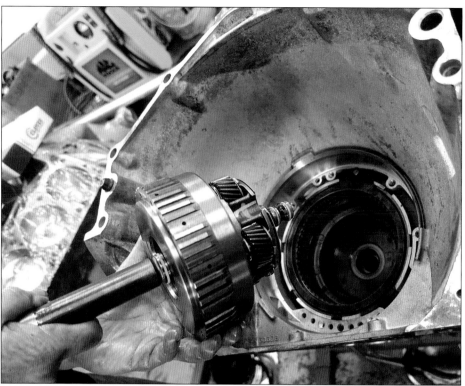

4 *The turbine shaft and overrun clutch housing assembly can now be lowered slowly through the fourth-gear clutch set.*

5 *Denny used his Vise-Grips to rotate the turbine shaft to check for engagement from fore to aft in all the shafts. The rear output shaft should rotate, ensuring that they are connected.*

Dropping the Third Gear Clutch into the 4L80E

1 The direct clutch housing and intermediate clutch race can now be put back and installed into the transmission. The gear on top should be able to spin clockwise and not be able to turn counterclockwise. Check for no interference before dropping in the direct clutch housing.

2 The front band assembly is shown in its correct orientation and seated properly. There is a small notch in the case that will locate the band snuggly.

3 The direct clutch housing gets placed in first and must align with the clutch pack already in the case.

4 To get the positioning just right, sometimes it requires rotating the entire assembly for better reach and maneuverability.

There is a proper tool to pull and lower the direct clutch housing (part number J38733 for the direct clutch installer/remover). If you don't have that on hand, a pair of picks work just fine.

Fourth Clutch Assembly

The fourth clutch assembly is self-explanatory. It functions just as the name implies: it is the fourth gear of the transmission, which is more colloquially known as overdrive. Overhauling the fourth clutch assembly is not always necessary, and most people do not bother taking it apart. However, in the uncommon instance where that is needed, the component comes apart easily.

To overhaul this assembly, remove the snap ring that holds in the spring and retainer assembly by compressing the spring-retainer ring. Inspect and clean all components thoroughly before reassembling them.

The piston and housing will separate once the snap ring is removed. There is a seal between the piston and spring retainer that rarely needs replacing but can be a source of bleeding fluid, so check to make sure that it's still in good shape before putting the fourth clutch housing in the case.

The clutches can be installed inside or outside of the case. It's a matter of preference. We choose for purposes of demonstration to do it with the clutches outside the case. We installed the fourth clutch housing by itself.

Installing the clutches outside the case allows us to check for clearance between the backing plate and the snap ring. This clearance should be between 0.040 and 0.100 inch, respectively, using a feeler gauge. Keep in mind that the small tang on the thicker backing plate must align with the case-locating pin and the fourth clutch housing center support bolt that is located in the oil passages on the bottom of the case.

The fourth clutch housing is put into place in the case without much fanfare, but make sure that the center support bolt hole is aligned properly to the case. Otherwise, the bolt will not be able to be torqued properly. You should not have to work to get the bolt in or out.

Make sure to torque this bolt, which is located on the fluid-passage side (in the bottom valve body area), to 12 ft-lbs. This is only to hold the carrier in place, so do not overtorque it. Otherwise, you may damage the case.

The overdrive unit and output shaft can be lowered into place to check for alignment and depth. If any singular component is not seated properly, the 4L80E will not go back together properly. Finding that piece can be frustrating at times. It's best to check your work at every stage to catch minor errors.

Always presoak all of the parts prior to install. This goes double for clutch friction plates, which can absorb much more than the solid-steel plates. To install the clutches, there are four steel plate discs and four clutch friction discs.

Start with a seal first and then a clutch steel disc, and alternate friction discs and steel discs until they run out. The final plate is a thick steel plate with teeth called the fourth clutch backing plate. This plate is held in with a snap ring and has a large, very noticeable tang on one side, locating it to the case. Make sure that the snap ring is fully seated before moving forward. Otherwise, it may interfere with alignment in the next phase.

Overdrive Unit Assembly

The overdrive unit is essentially the same as the rest of the gear drive

Reassembling the Overdrive Unit Assembly

1 The rear drive carrier assembly has this thrust washer between mating surfaces.

2 The overrun clutch assembly has a new roller bearing slid into place.

3 Inside the overrun clutch assembly are these three large sets of clutch plates. The old clutch pack is on the left and looking a little used.

4 Always douse the parts that you are about to install in new transmission fluid for a smooth first start.

5 *Every clutch pack in virtually any automatic transmission will alternate the disc and steel rings. These are referred to as a clutch steels or plates and a wearable clutch discs.*

6 *The clutch pack is topped off with a thicker clutch pressure plate that is different than the rest of the group. That will be the top part that is held in by the snap ring shown here.*

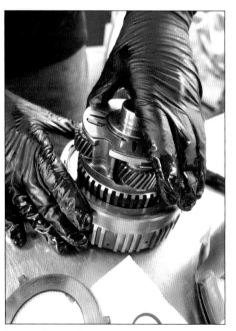

7 *The planetary gearset and overrun clutch housing assembly can now go back together.*

assemblies that we have rebuilt up until this point with the exception that this includes the input shaft (also called the turbine shaft) and a set of planetary gears on the business end. Inside the overrun clutch housing is a piston, revise spring carrier, and a clutch pack just like the rest of the assemblies we've tackled. So, this will be very familiar by now.

Begin by removing the snap ring from the input shaft near the planetaries. The carrier assembly slides off the shaft easily without much effort. Remember to remove the green O-ring on the engine side of the shaft. Without removing this O-ring, the shaft cannot be removed; even though it is small, it makes a big difference.

The overdrive carrier with planetaries can be separated from the overrun clutch housing at this point, exposing the clutch stack and the overdrive roller bearing. Next, remove the snap ring that holds in the clutch discs and steel plates. In this stack are three alternating clutch steel plates and three clutch friction discs. Again, compress the spring stack and remove the corresponding snap ring. You have had plenty of practice with this, so it will be second nature.

From here, remove the overrun clutch piston from the overrun clutch housing. Make sure to clean and inspect all parts thoroughly for damage and cleanliness. If the piston is damaged or appears in poor shape, replace it at this juncture.

If it needs replacing, then use an Assemblee Goo to the molded

Adding New Clutches and Seals to the Carrier Assembly

1 *Throughout this entire process, things may not line up well due to the clutch packs being misaligned. Carefully use a small, flat-blade screwdriver to align them and slide the part into place. A little shimmying back and forth will help, but do not force them together.*

2 *Denny feels for engagement as he drops the planetary gearset into place through each of the clutch discs.*

3 *This is the proper depth of engagement to look for.*

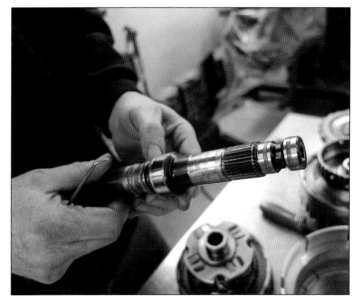

4 *This shaft runs through the overrun clutch and overdrive assembly and is called the turbine shaft. A number of hard but malleable plastic rings encircle it. Not replacing these now may cause fluid leakage into the wrong chambers.*

seal portion and, keeping the piston level, rotate the piston into place. Do not use any cleaner on the piston rubber. Otherwise, it may cause it to crack and malfunction.

If the piston is still good, wipe it clean and reinstall it. Do not use chemicals to clean it. Now, install the snap right and remove the spring compressor.

As with the other assemblies, there will be a series of alternating clutches and clutch discs. Starting with a steel plate, place it inside the housing and replace the worn friction discs with new ones every other disc much like before. However, this time there will be only three clutch steel discs and three clutch friction discs, whereas the others had many more. This is the major reason why the overdrive gear is usually the weakest gear in any transmission. In reality, there doesn't need to be much force to keep a car at speed, so switching to a lower gear to maintain speed is not taxing on the unit.

Once the clutch pack is assembled, replace the snap ring and check the clearance with a feeler gauge between the snap ring and the clutch backing plate. Proper clearance will be between 0.033 and 0.094 inch between the two pieces.

We move next to the carrier assembly with the planetaries installed. These assemblies do not generally need to be taken apart to have parts replaced. In our case, this is exactly what happened. There was no excessive heat or wear that was noticeable after a close inspection and cleaning. It is not recommended to rebuild the carrier assembly unless it is totally necessary. However, if you need to, there is a large snap ring holding in the entire assembly together, and it has a number of washers and needle bearings for each planetary gear.

Make sure to note the top of each pinion gear and the location of it in relation to the carrier so that it can be reinstalled properly in the exact orientation from whence it came. Failure to do so will result in poor performance or potentially terminal damage to the 4L80E.

Moving on to the turbine shaft, there is an official installation tool

This is the fourth clutch case bolt. Use a 40 torx bit and torque it to 12 ft-lbs.

Replacing the Plastic Shaft Seals

1 *The new plastic rings stretch a bit to accommodate the larger bore size of the turbine shaft.*

2 *The new rings (bottom in white) are shown. Compare them to the old worn out rings (top and black) that were brittle and broke when taken off.*

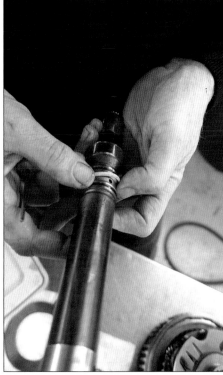

3 *The rings will slide on easily enough but will not spring back like a rubber ring would.*

4 *Denny used a worm gear to tighten up the rings and form them into place.*

5 *The turbine shaft is now ready to be sent home. Note the vertical orientation.*

7 *Denny explained that having a few of these large holes in his metal table would come in handy because you can use them to prop up your assemblies. This will keep them steady while you put them together.*

6 *This snap ring will retain the shaft in place.*

for the seals (part number J-38736), which comes with a number of different parts to aid in the installation of said seals. However, for the $200 asking price for the tool, you may as well just buy another 4L80E from the junkyard. We cannot justify the cost when a very cheap alternative is already available in most people's garages.

If you rebuild transmissions on a daily basis, there might be an argument to have the specific tools for various sizes, but a 30-cent worm-gear clamp suffices to snug down the nylon seals to the turbine shaft. We recommend starting with the bottom seal and working your way up the shaft because it's easier to manipulate the seals into place.

Once the is shaft ready, replace the roller clutch bearing and install the carrier into the clutch housing. Make sure to align all the clutch steel plates and clutch friction discs carefully. Next, slip the turbine shaft through the carrier splines without nicking or damaging the seals in the process.

Finally, install the snap ring at the bottom of the assembly with

Aftermarket center supports with oversized pistons apply more clamping force on clutches for high-horsepower applications and less slippage.

the small end of the turbine shaft sticking out the bottom. The thrust bearing will need to be coated in Assemblee Goo and installed with the silver side facing up during the reinstallation of the overdrive clutch assembly. Ensure that the unit is fully seated into the case before moving on to the oil pump.

Oil Pump

Not all oil pumps will need to be fully rebuilt, but since you are already this far, it won't hurt to put in a bit of sweat equity into it. Besides, if you're diligent about maintenance, you won't have to do this for another 300,000 miles.

In our case, the Monster Transmission kit included a shift kit for the 4L80E, which should firm up the shifts, make shifts feel more consistent, eliminate converter shudder, and prevent premature failure of the unit.

To separate the two halves of the oil pump, we removed the five M8 1.25x40 bolts on the back side of the

This piece is not native to a stock 4L80E. This is a snap-ring pressure apply, which is an aftermarket piece. It is used to keep pressure on the snap ring under severe loads.

These are the old internal parts that will be replaced. There are many potential failure and wear points.

Separating the Oil Pump

1 Moving on to the shift kit, begin by removing the oil pump body from the cover with a series of bolts.

2 The inside of the oil pump body shows the pump drive gears with a half-moon-shaped divider. It is important to remember that all identification marks must be facing upward when reassembling.

3 Here we have more oil-ring seals that are plastic and form fit with a worm gear clamped around the outside.

4 Denny has an unorthodox method to remove the front pump seal: a seal puller with a few hammer blows and a well-placed knee for downward pressure.

5 *The pressure regulator valve comes out once this snap ring is removed.*

pump with a mini impact gun. The front half holds the two gears that make up the pump itself.

The smaller inner gear rotates from the power of the engine, and the larger gear is driven by that gear to generate power and create oil pressure via the crescent moon–shaped

hardened metal piece between them. These need to be cleaned and inspected for damage and put back into the front half of the pump with Assemblee Goo holding them in place. It's now ready for the first start-up.

There are identification marks on both gears, so when it is time to put them back, make sure the marks are facing up. If you are inclined to check proper spacing, place a straightedge over the front pump face and gearset and measure for proper clearance (0.0007 to 0.0028 inch). For most typical rebuilds, this is a non-factor.

To complete the front-half rebuild, the front oil pump seal will need to be yanked out of position and

Oil Pump Front Half Reconditioning

1 *The front pump seal (shown here) is not properly seated and will leak. It will need a little persuading (hit it firmly but evenly).*

2 *The old pump body bushing and new seal are taken out and put back in with the same method: an appropriate-size punch and a few blows with a hammer.*

3 *This is the oil-pump bushing. A few whacks with a hammer and flat-blade screwdriver pinned the new one in place.*

4 *The new rear stator shaft bushing is properly seated.*

5 *The oil-pump drive gears have been cleaned and reinstalled with Assemblee Goo.*

replaced. All kits will come with this seal; it is a must for any rebuild. Inside is a thick bushing that also should be replaced, regardless of how it looks. This can be removed with a hammer and a flat object, such as a screwdriver. Apply equal pressure around the bushing on the way out. You will replace it by using the proper bearing installation tool or a large socket.

On the back end of the rear half of the pump is another pair of nylon seals. They need to be pried from their resting place and replaced just like the other seals inside the 4L80E.

The oil pump has a number of valves, seals, and springs that all need refreshing and are similar in nature and design. Rather than detailing each one, we will discuss removal and refreshing as a concept and cover any differences that arise.

Each valve has either a roll pin or a snap ring that holds it in place. Removing the snap ring will release the valve, which will have a spring holding it in place. A few of them will have small discs locating and limiting the valve travel.

Our shift kit came with a few upgrade springs to replace old ones. It helps to do one valve at a time and line up the parts as they come out of the oil pump. Then, match up replacement parts from the kit and clean and inspect parts that are meant to be reused. We started with the reverse booster and worked our way around the pump, but you can start at any point.

Oil Pump Pressure Regulator Valve

1 Our shift kit from Monster Transmission came with a replacement for the reverse boost regulator. So, the old one is removed.

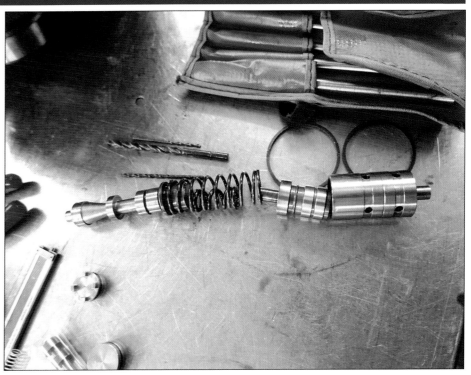

2 From left to right, the cone-shaped object is the pressure-regulator valve followed by two springs, a reverse boost valve, and the reverse boost bushing. This is in order in which they go back into the oil pump.

3 Our shift kit required a relief hole drilled into the pump body.

4 Our pump assembly got a new main seal, races, and a pressure regulator. It's ready to drop in.

There is nothing special to note here when taking apart the rest of the valves for inspection and cleaning. The only notes of value are to only do one at time, go slowly and methodically, and do not mix the parts up. Make sure to replace the main pump gasket in its proper orientation and finger-tighten the bolts back into place. Do not fully torque the bolts yet.

When you are ready to torque the oil-pump cover bolts, inspect all the small cup plugs on the top and sides of the pump to make sure that they are still in place. Use a large worm gear band to align the halves together to torque the five bolts to 18 ft-lbs.

A liberal amount of Assemblee Goo around the edges will help glide the pump back into place in the case. Also, lube the turbine shaft seals to make sure that they didn't bind when the pump was installed.

The oil pump requires a new gasket between the case and the pump assembly.

Reinstalling the Oil Pump

1 *Before shoving the pump home and essentially closing off the guts of the 4L80E, throw more Assemblee Goo on the edges for good measure.*

2 *The main input shaft also gets a liberal amount of Assemblee Goo.*

3 *The oil pump goes in with a very specific orientation. Denny dropped it in carefully to line up the bolt pattern. This will be snug and will immediately indicate if there is an alignment issue. Do not force the bolts in to snug the pump into place, as you risk damaging something internally.*

4 *Use a few mild hits with a dead-blow or other soft hammer to coerce the pump into place.*

5 *Once the pump is back in its final home, reinstall the input shaft O-ring. Remember that little nasty thing that prevented the pump from coming apart?*

The six pump-to-case bolts can be cinched down to 18 ft-lbs of torque.

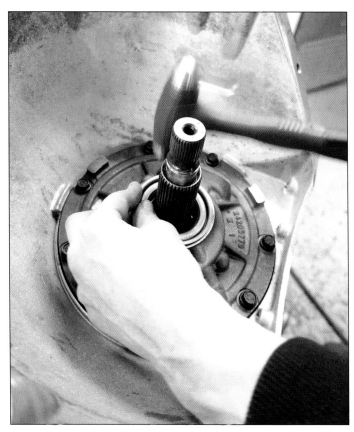

A new front pump seal is gently massaged into place.

Before gently lowering the pump into the case, remember to replace the selective thrust washer between the oil pump and the overdrive clutch housing. Always use a new oil pump cover gasket to seal the pump from leaks.

Because all of the seals and gasket are new, the pump may need a few gentle smacks with the butt of a hammer to get fully seated. The pump bolts are clocked in such a manner that it is almost impossible to install incorrectly, but the pump will need to be pressed into place in most cases. Make sure to replace the turbine shaft O-ring, lubricate it, and torque the mounting bolts to 18 ft-lbs of force.

Rotate the turbine shaft while cinching down the bolts from the pump to the case to ensure that the overrun, fourth clutch, forward, and direct clutch houses have been installed properly. This is mainly due to clutch discs not being fully engaged before full assembly. If the turbine cannot be rotated, the entire assembly must be taken apart and fully aligned. Simply torquing down the case bolts on the oil pump will not solve the issue and will lead to catastrophic failure of the 4L80E.

Most people do not have a dial indicator and do not check the end play of the turbine shaft. However, if you have a dial indicator and you wish to check the turbine shaft's end play, install the dial indicator on the bellhousing with the indicator set to zero on the end of the turbine shaft. Manually, pull out the turbine shaft and subtract that from the overdrive carrier play.

The permissible allowance is 0.004 to 0.022 inch of play. If this is out of spec, change the selective washer between the oil pump and the overdrive assembly. Some kits provide the following thicknesses; some do not. If yours has more than one, here is a quick guide reference for thicknesses.

Blue Stripe: 0.057–0.061 inch
Red Stripe: 0.073–0.077 inch
Brown Stripe: 0.089–0.093 inch
Green Stripe: 0.105–0.109 inch
No Stripe: 0.121–0.125 inch

If you decided to check the end play of the turbine shaft, you will probably be interested in the end play of the tailshaft. Using a dial indicator holder on the six-bolt tail section, measure the end play of the output shaft by pulling it in and out. Proper end play should be 0.005 to 0.025 inch. If end play is not achieved, a replacement shim should be replaced at the back of the transmission, which means taking it all apart and putting it all back together.

With all that sorted, the internal section of the 4L80E build is complete. Rotate the unit so that the valve body and oil passages are facing up because there is a fair amount of work to be done in this section.

Shift Kit Modifications

Our shift kit required us to perform a few modifications to the pump itself and the valve body area by drilling some relief holes. The kit supplied the appropriate drill bits and provided detailed instructions for where to drill. If you choose the straight rebuild process, this step is not necessary and may compromise the function of the 4L80E. This is an all-or-nothing type of procedure.

Shift kits are all slightly different, so follow all of the procedures for yours. Our kit required removal of a small bit of material from the crescent-pump shape. Thankfully, ours was already done at the factory. Keep in mind that our kit was specific to our year and model, so make sure to specify the exact build date of yours to get the right kit—not all are the

Our shift kit came with a couple drill bits to assist in the installation. The valve body plate gets a hole enlarged.

same or broken down by early or late.

The first thing that our kit instructed us to do was to drill a drainback passage in the oil pump face. When drilling holes, make sure to clean up any debris or metal shavings, as this contamination is a big failure risk.

Our kit from Monster Transmission included a replacement pressure regulator valve and the related springs for the oil pump. It also replaced the boost valve, shoulder washer, and sleeve. It required a few holes to be drilled in the valve body

Our shift kit came with the required drill bit and diagram to drill the respective hole. It's best to do this with the case vertical so you don't introduce metal shavings into the case.

separator plate, provided specific sizes to drill, and noted where the holes should go. It even included the correct-size drill bits in the kit.

Next, the kit's instructions stated to remove and replace the shift solenoid filter that was included in the kit. It also came with a bore plug and new O-ring, but the original roll pin was reused. Following that, inside the valve body, the TCC regulator valve was replaced with the anti-shudder version that was in the kit.

Since we had a late-style case (1997 and up), we had to drill a 3/16-inch hole in a small part of the oil passage, which was located by the instruction guide. Also, as old lore would have it, our kit required a small modification to the check balls in the oil-passage gallery by removing one on the far bottom; yours may vary.

Intermediate Servo Piston

The bottom of the transmission rebuild begins with the intermediate servo piston. The rebuild kit should come with a new seal to snug around the piston. Secure the E-clip to the piston pin and push this assembly into the appropriate receptacle with the spring first, then the spring retainer, and then the piston. This should engage with the intermediate band. It will be loose until the rebuilt valve body is installed.

Reverse Servo

From the intermediate servo, now replace the reverse servo and the accumulator assembly. Start by installing the servo retainer on the pin with both springs and top it off with the washer. When

Pictured here is the correct assembly order for the reverse servo and 1-2 accumulator assembly. When assembled, torque the cover retaining bolts to 18 ft-lbs.

replacing the seal on the rear accumulator servo, place it over the pin and springs with inner and outer oil ring seals.

Cap this off with the rear servo piston and the small E-clip. To clamp it all down with a new reverse servo cover gasket, place the reverse servo cover over the rear servo piston and snug down the six retaining bolts to 18 ft-lbs.

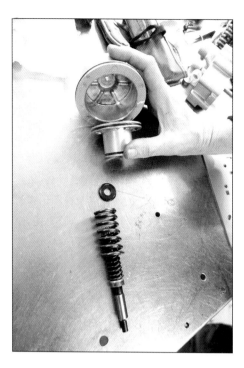

Reinstalling the Reverse Servo

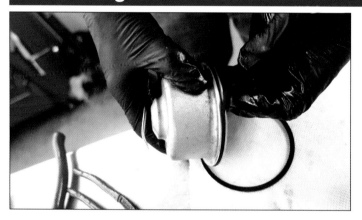

1 *Our rear servo piston also received a new O-ring gasket. It's always a good idea to replace these, even if the old ones seem good.*

2 *Our rear servo piston (left) and the rear accumulator piston (right) are cleaned with new seals and are now ready for assembly.*

3 *The rear servo housing has its own thin metal plate gasket that only has one way that it goes on.*

4 *The rear servo housing gets bolted to 18 ft-lbs on each bolt.*

Clutch Piston Engagement Check

Denny at Sharadon Performance in Hugo, Minnesota, uses compressed air to check the clutch and piston engagement of each gear. Because fluid and air dynamics work very similarly, especially in this case, Denny showed us a way to engage each gear with a short piece of rubber hose and compressed air.

Air Checking Piston Engagement

1 *Denny blows a short blast of compressed air into this port on the case side of the valve body veins. He listens carefully for a small popping noise that indicates that the internal assembly is getting proper engagement.*

2 *Denny uses compressed air to check for engagement of the reverse clutch. There is a slight popping noise when it engages with medium air pressure, simulating normal hydraulic pressure.*

3 *The same technique is applied to the other reverse port on the case, which is located where Denny has his air nozzle.*

Holding the tube tightly against the oil passage in cavity number 43, Denny blew a short burst of air, listened carefully, and felt the case for a popping noise that indicated that the reverse gear was engaging under pressure. The noise is a bit faint, but it is very distinct, like rubber hitting metal and reverting back to its original position once the pressure is released. This is also a very good demonstration of how an automatic transmission works.

This can be done for number 24 for the second clutch, number 43 for the third clutch, and number 37 for the overdrive clutch (fourth gear).

Valve Body

Think of the valve body in any transmission as the brains of the operation. Even before there were computers, electronic solenoids, and sensors galore, there was the valve body. Modern transmissions still have them, as they function as impressive feats of engineering. The design work and casting that goes into them is a sight to behold.

Our 4L80E rebuild of the internals is complete, and it is ready to be rotated in the horizontal position.

This is the case side of the valve body. Just looking at the array and ports has caused many a mechanic great confusion. It certainly is a marvel how this was created. Before assembly and marveling at your handywork, check the torque specs on both carrier bolts as well as the cleanliness of the passages and case before moving forward.

The Valve Body Plate

1 All rebuild kits will come with a replacement valve body gasket. It only goes on one way.

2 Unbolting the accumulator housing is a non-affair. However, note of the length of bolts because they are not all the same. There are two distinct versions: long and short.

3 All rebuild kits come with an accumulator gasket, just like ours did from Monster Transmission.

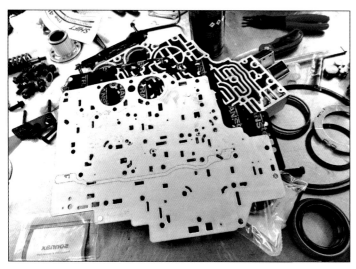

You probably discovered that there is a spacer plate between the valve body and the transmission case. There are two gaskets that need to sandwich this plate. Ours (pictured) was a Trans-go plate that was installed by the previous owner.

We start reconditioning the valve body by laying it out on the bench and laying down more paper towels. There will be transmission fluid still inside, and it will come out.

The valve body plates are complex and often the weak link in the longevity of the transmission itself. Precomputer tweaks to older models usually involved a shift kit, such as we've done here, or modification to the torque converter.

Think of tuning the valve body as being akin to tuning an old-school carburetor. And yet, with all of the electronic items, there are still some elements that can change the behavior of the transmission, as we've discussed briefly in our shift kit installation.

When going through the valve body, focus on one component at a time to keep track of all the parts and not mix them together. There will be a number of roll pins, springs, valves, and solenoids that can easily end up in the wrong location if care and precision are not used.

When all of the parts are removed, lay them out in the exact order in which they came out. Clean and dry them thoroughly before reinstallation. Once all of the pieces are removed from the valve body

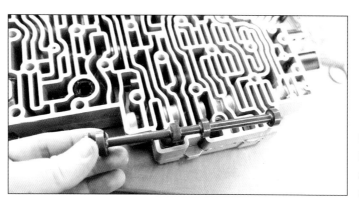

This is the manual valve inside the valve body. It is located here and in this orientation.

itself, clean it with your favorite solvent and then blow the unit completely dry with an air compressor. Even after we cleaned ours, we found some dirt and debris by wiping it with a clean towel.

First Things First

The first and easiest item to fix is the force motor feed filter screen, which pops in and out with a little bit of force using your fingers or a small tool. Ours was not completely blocked and is probably still usable, but it's better to be safe than sorry, so it was replaced.

From there, we removed the roll pin from the 3-4 shift valve check-ball plug location and replaced it with one from our kit. Our kit came with a new valve and check-ball plug as part of the kit, but most replacement kits will not have replacement valves, as they are meant to be reused.

Changing valves will change the behavior of the transmission by allowing differing levels of fluid at differing times based on the valve shape and size. Think of valves as timing devices that can adjust timing and fluid volume.

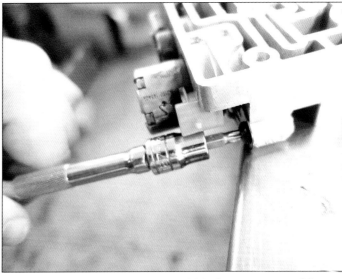

Often overlooked, the force motor feed filter screen needs to be replaced. Notice the small particulates that it captured when comparing the new filter screen (left) with the old (right).

The variable force motor solenoid bolt comes out with a T27 torx head socket.

Variable Force Motor

From there, our attention turns to the variable force motor (VFM). It is held in with a T27 torx bit and a Y-shaped tensioned-clip-style clamp. Our Monster Transmission kit came with a new one, and it was good that it did because the screen on our old one appeared to be completely clogged with metal shavings. If your rebuild kit does not have one, cleaning the screen with solvent and drying it with light compressed air will suffice.

PWM Solenoid

The next piece alongside the VFM is the PWM solenoid. This is retained by a small plastic clip inside the valve body oil passages. A small pick makes quick work of removing the solenoid. Our kit came with a replacement PWM solenoid. This is common in kits that cost a bit more, as they tend to be more comprehensive in the parts they supply. This is no exception to the, "buy once, cry once" philosophy.

Behind this is a roll pin that is difficult to access, as it only has one way to remove it: upward. There is no corresponding hole on the other side to drive out the pin, so a pair of long, slender needle-nose pliers was needed to get enough grip on the pin to remove it. Once purchase has been gained on the roll pin, it can be removed from the top. This pin holds in the TCC regulator valve and TCC spring.

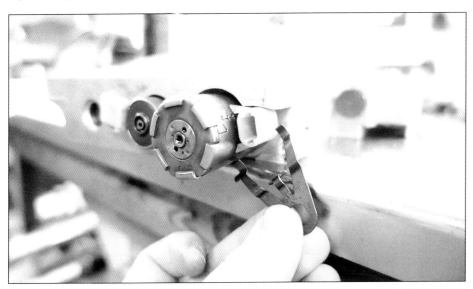

Once the screw is out, there is a retaining clip that holds the solenoid in place.

The PWM solenoid is held in by this retaining clip. A sharp pick or small screwdriver will pry it loose.

Unless your 4L80E was experiencing issues, this does not generally need to be removed—unless you are a completionist and want to clean every inch of the valve body. While it is not completely necessary, it is recommended to remove it and make sure that the spring and valve are clean and intact.

Compare the old (right) and new (left) PWM solenoids.

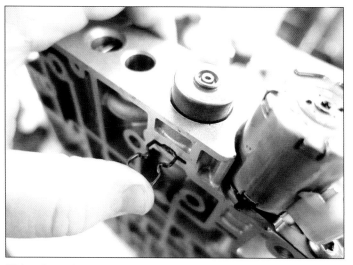

This clip to hold the PWM will click into place. Don't force it too much; it will sit flush with the valve body.

Installing a Roll Pin

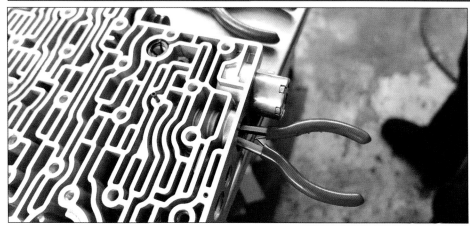

1 This particular roll pin is located smack-dab in the middle of the valve body and only has one hole, so pushing it from the backside is impossible. This oddball pair of pliers that Denny had on hand was the only one that was long and skinny enough with enough grip to get any purchase on the pin. Behind this roll pin is the torque convertor clutch (TCC) regulator apply valve and spring.

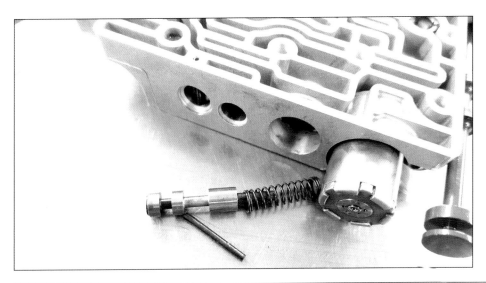

2 *Here is the TCC regulator apply valve and spring.*

The next two holes beside the PWM hold the actuator feed limit valve and accumulator valve, respectively. Each are held in with a roll pin that comes out easily with a small punch and a few taps of a hammer. Each has a plug and a corresponding spring that should not be interchanged.

As with the other components, inspect them for damage, clean them

This coiled spring roll pin holds the check ball plug and check ball behind it. It can be tapped out from either direction.

The PWM solenoid is held in by a retaining clip that is easily removed with a flat-blade screwdriver.

Here is the check ball and plug.

thoroughly, and use compressed air to completely dry the pieces. Align the pieces on a clean, dry surface before reinstallation.

Rotating the valve body 180 degrees, the same approach is taken with the side as with the rest. Disassemble each component, and then clean, dry, and reinstall them.

On the far left is a check ball and sleeve (big roll pin). Remove and fully clean them before drying and reinstallation.

Shift Solenoids

The next item (next to the "A" shift solenoid) is the shift solenoid

feed filter and plug. The stock configuration is a plug with a small spring behind the filter for the late model. Our shift kit replaced this with a new plug and a smaller filter. We needed to change ours anyway, as it was almost completely covered in dirt and debris.

Not all kits will come with

Shift Solenoids and Shift Valves

1 *There is a difference in solenoid styles. We received the wrong variant and ordered a replacement. The correct style will largely depend on the wiring harness version.*

2 *The old solenoid had a fair amount of metal shavings caught in the tight mesh filter, so it was definitely time for a replacement.*

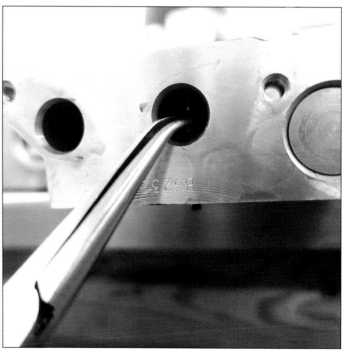

3 *The valve body has a few instances where you'll need to remove a roll pin to access certain parts. This is not always required for all rebuilds, but note that a few only come out in one direction.*

4 Once the roll pin is poking out slightly, a quick prying action with a pair of angled needle-nose pliers will do the trick.

5 This is the 1-2 shift valve. The middle hole pictured here is its home, and the orientation with the spring going into the hole first is the correct alignment.

6 Behind the 1-2 shift solenoid lies a roll pin that houses the 1-2 shift valve and spring.

replacement 1-2 and 2-3 shift sole-noids. While they generally can be reused in most cases, we advise replacing them since you've already come this far. They are held in with T27 torx head bolts and are often labeled shift solenoid A and shift solenoid B.

The A solenoid is blue and the B solenoid is red, which is another way to distinguish them. With the accumulator cup facing up, the solenoid on the left is A (blue) and the one on the right is B (red) if the colors are faded or you've mixed them up.

Rebuilding the Valves within the Valve Body

1 A small punch set is needed to remove the roll pin holding in this check ball plug.

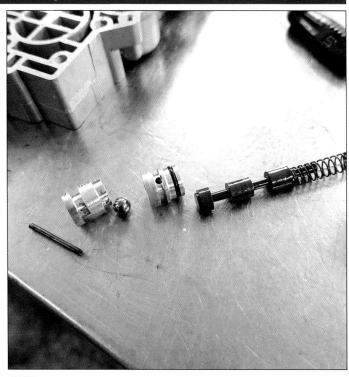

2 Behind the check ball plug resides the 3-4 shift valve and shift valve return spring for the 2-3 and 3-4 shifts.

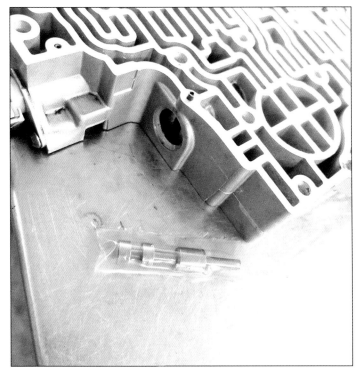

3 Our shift kit came with a new 3-4 shift valve. It goes in pointy side first.

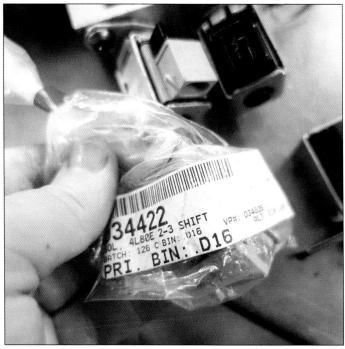

4 Our 2-3 shift solenoid came labeled in the bag. Despite there being a visual color difference, it's worth keeping them separate and swapping them one at a time.

5 Swapping solenoids is not always necessary. They often will work just fine for hundreds of thousands of miles. Since we'd come this far, we used the new ones.

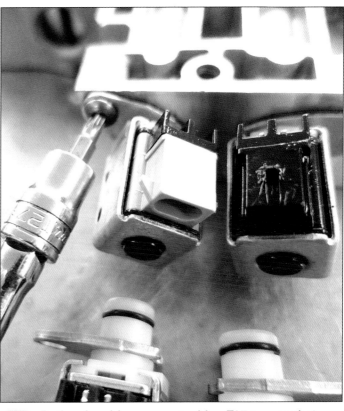

6 Both solenoids come out with a T27 torx socket.

7 Another coiled roll pin is located next to the 1-2 shift solenoid. It holds in the shift solenoid feed filter and filter plug. This can be pressed out from either side of the valve body.

8 Sometimes the filter and plug are stuck inside and need to a little coaxing from a pick.

9 The old filter, spring, and plug (lower set) were almost completely clogged, so we were glad we replaced it with the new set (upper set) that came with our shift kit. Notice how it has a smaller filter body and has a metal O-ring sealed base.

10 In this case, we improvised and used a 1/4-inch extension to push the piece back through the valve body.

Once you are satisfied with your assessment and cleaning of the valve body, it is time to overhaul and install the accumulator housing.

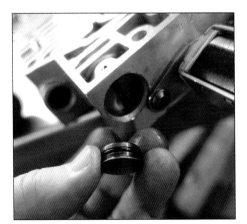

11 This will be a very snug fit, so don't be surprised when you feel some tension. The O-rings are new and not worn in yet, which will give some feedback.

The valve body has a metal spacer, which is shown hovering above the case. Between the spacer and the case is a gasket that is easily identified because it is wholly different from the valve body to spacer gasket.

When removing the accumulator housing, inside will be two plastic pistons like this one.

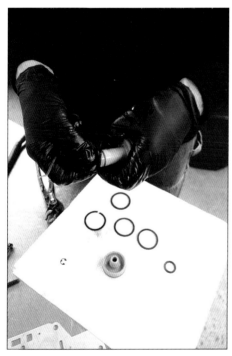

Denny sets out to recondition the accumulator pistons with new O-rings. A standard rebuild kit will come with these, just as our Monster Transmission set did.

There are two different variants, so keep them straight. For reference, the right side pictured here is the fourth gear clutch accumulator and the one on the left is for the third gear clutch.

Accumulator Housing

The accumulator housing has its own cast-aluminum housing, two pistons, and three springs with a host of seals that need to be replaced. Start by removing the springs and laying them in order on the bench. The left side will house the third clutch accumulator piston and spring. The similar-size piston on the right will be the fourth clutch accumulator piston.

The fourth clutch accumulator piston is held in with a spring just like the third clutch piston, but it has a large piston pin driven through the middle. The smaller hole to the right is the torque signal compensator valve and the related spring.

The spring goes first, then the piston, which is opposite for the third and fourth clutch accumulator pistons, where the pistons are behind their respective springs. Replace the square-cut 1.615-inch seals around each piston, and then clean, dry, and reassemble them.

Once the accumulator housing assembly has been completed and you are ready to install it, replace the valve body to spacer gasket onto the valve body (the side that faces the oil passages). Then, lay the spacer on top of that along with the accumulator housing gasket. Finally, top it all off with the spacer plate-to-case gasket and install the newly refurbished accumulator housing. Hand tighten all of the bolts.

Reinstalling the Front Servo Piston

1 *Our rear accumulator piston gets new O-ring seals.*

3 Our front servo piston also sports a new O-ring.

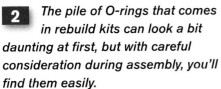

2 The pile of O-rings that comes in rebuild kits can look a bit daunting at first, but with careful consideration during assembly, you'll find them easily.

4 The front servo piston gets lubed up and put into the case after a new seal. The front servo piston will need the associated spring (not pictured).

Accumulator Housing Bolts

1 Once the accumulator housing has been rebuilt and the piston has been replaced, it's good to check for correct fitment and orientation before torqueing down the bolts.

2 The accumulator body is held in by two different length bolts. There are five short ones and one long one. The long one goes where the bolt you see in the accumulator body is currently located. These bolts are torqued to 97 in-lbs.

3 *These bolts also have different-size heads, which is another way to distinguish them.*

Reinstalling the Accumulator Housing

1 *The accumulator case will receive its own special gasket between it and the valve body spacer. This photo demonstrates the assembly without springs shown.*

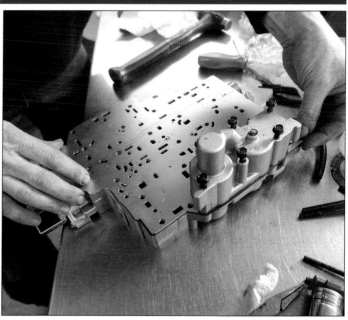

2 *The accumulator goes over the valve body metal plate spacer with the accumulator gasket between the two.*

Note the position of the longer bolt; the other five bolts are shorter in length. The longer bolt will be located directly between the fourth clutch accumulator piston hole and the torque signal compensator valve opening. It will also have a taller standoff built into the accumulator housing casting.

Now, torque all accumulator bolts to 97 in-lbs in a clockwise circular pattern, starting with the middle bolt between the third and fourth clutch pistons on the edge of the valve body.

3 *Using five standard-size bolts and one longer one, torque the accumulator bolts to 98 in-lbs.*

Valve Body Bolt Placement

1 *The valve body metal spacer has a gasket between it and the valve body itself. There are two similar but distinct valve body gaskets.*

2 *The valve body gasket rests in place, ready for the valve body assembly.*

3 *Denny carefully lowers the completed valve body onto the gasket, making sure to line up the bolt holes with caution.*

4 *The accumulator pump has two distinct bolt sizes: long and short. There are five short bolts and one long bolt. The long bolt is located here, noted by the lower right bolt not being tightened down.*

Reinstalling the Manual Shift Shaft and Parking Lock Actuator

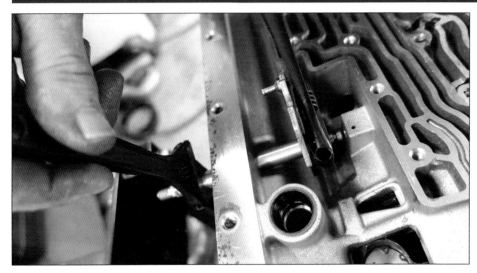

1 *The manual shift shaft requires two wrenches to tighten the lock bolt on the inside of the case. Note that the detent on the lever plate is backward and should be facing inward toward the case. We corrected this when we noticed our error.*

2 *Before installing the shift shaft, attach the parking lock bar. The parking actuator assembly should sit easily in the case.*

4 The shifter shaft has a very small nail-like pin that has grooves along the sides. You were warned to keep this piece safe, as it's easy to lose. Drive this into the hole with light taps to lock the shaft into place. Tap just enough to ensure that it has enough bite and will not wiggle out, but do not over tap.

3 The parking lock bracket can go back on with the M8 1.2x20 bolt.

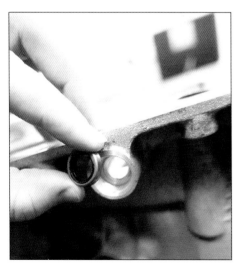

Our rebuild kit came with this shift lever arm seal. This is pressed in until flush with the case.

The parking lock bracket goes back in finger tight before final torque down.

Retainer Pin

We found that installing the interior detent assembly (positive detent shifter plate) and parking lock actuator prior to the valve body gave us more room to work. Note the orientation of the pin in the detent plate, as it needs to align with the main shift valve in the valve body. This includes the parking lock bracket and the manual shift shaft with the nail-like pin that retains the shaft. Tap this down to secure it, but do not pound this in too far.

At this point, it might be easier to install a new wiring harness, as accessing the outside port is a bit easier. We found that lubing up the seal will aid in allowing the plug to slip into place easier because the new seal tends to be larger and less pliable than an old shrunken brittle seal.

Installing the Shift Detent Forward and Backward

1 We discovered that the shifter detent plate can in fact go in the wrong way. The transmission would not shift if we left it as is.

2 Here is the shifter detent properly installed and residing within the manual shifter valve. This should move freely.

3 The shift lever arm is held in place with a small pin-like nail with serrated edges. A few small taps with a hammer (until it cannot be pulled out) will keep it secured.

4 The parking pawl return spring is latched upon this stud that is built into the case and around the parking lock pawl.

5 The manual detent is now installed with M6 1.0x55 bolts. It gets bolted to 18 ft-lbs of torque.

7 The parking pawl shaft is held in with this retaining clip. If you do not intend to remove the parking pawl or shaft, leave this in place. Most rebuilds do not take this step.

6 This is pretty hard to mess up, but make sure that the detent rests inside one of the notches of the detent plate.

When it comes time to replace the check balls in the case, an easy way to keep them in place is a dap of Assemblee Goo. It's sticky and provides lubrication for the first start-up.

These are the stock locations of all eight check balls for the case, as indicated with blue Assemblee Goo. The eighth check ball is located in the lower right and is awaiting Assemblee Goo.

Another clue to the puzzle was this high-pressure relief assembly that the previous owner had installed as part of a TransGo basic shift kit. We put it back as we found it just in case because it seemed important. These kits were popular for a while to extend longevity of the 4L80E, as it tended to have line pressure that was too high in reverse gear, which would break the low-reverse band.

 TECH TIP

Gasket Placement

If the gaskets are too difficult to hold while lining up the valve body, either hold them with a small dab of Assemblee Goo or place them on the oil passage on the case and gently lower the valve body to ensure that the holes line up properly before cinching down the valve body bolts. ∎

Once that is complete, flip the valve body and drop it onto the 4L80E case. Be sure that the check balls are securely in place.

After you've successfully lowered the valve body onto its location, it's important to note that many bolts have dual purposes, including holding down other components. The PSM, detent spring, dipstick stop, crossover lube tube, and roller, along with three wire clips, all

PSM and Valve Body Bolts

1 Here is our old PSM (left) and the new one supplied in the Monster Transmission kit (right).

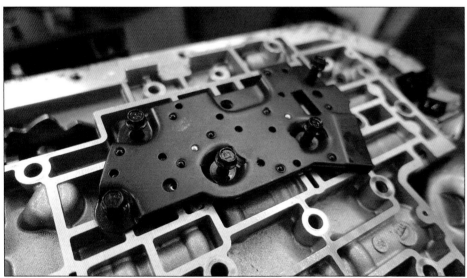

2 The PSM is installed next with M6 1.0 bolts. This also gets snugged down to 98 in-lbs.

3 Here we see two different sizes of bolts for the valve body. The standard bolt is an M6 1.0x55 (right), but there is one special bolt (left) that has a different head. Note this bolt is designed to go in the hole pictured that has no bolt in it, adjacent to the accumulator molds.

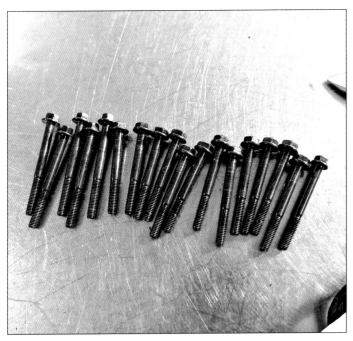

4 The valve body has a series of "regular" bolts and one special bolt. These can be reused during a rebuild unless one is broken.

5 Denny starts each bolt lightly and makes sure that all are aligned properly before torqueing them all down to 98 in-lbs. No special torque pattern is required.

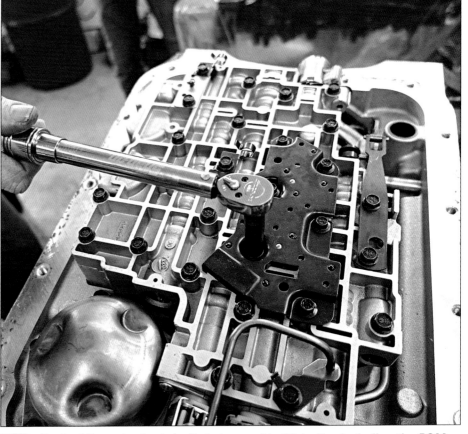

6 The other side of the lube tube is press fit into its location.

7 Each of the valve body bolts is torqued to 98 in-lbs, including the PSM.

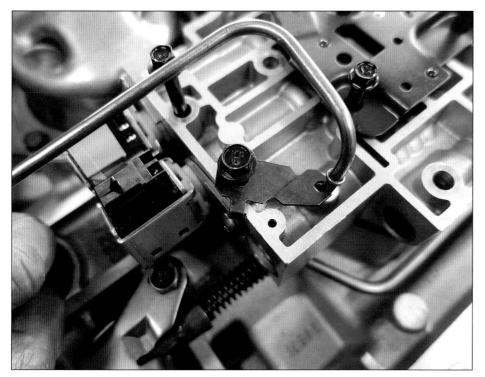

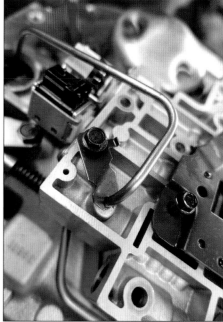

This oil crossover lube tube is pressed in and held down by this retainer clip.

The oil crossover tube is installed with the metal plate strip on the outside of the rolled edge.

use existing valve-body holes. From there, there will be 21 other bolts that need to be hand tightened. Each bolt gets snugged down to 116 in-lbs of torque.

Wiring Harness

Always use a new wiring harness when rebuilding your 4L80E. The chances of the old one becoming brittle over time and having a failure is a higher probability than it's worth for the price of a new harness. Most kits come with them, so make sure you specify which unit model you have because they are not interchangeable.

If the exterior bulkhead has been installed already, move on to snaking the wiring harness into place over the valve body. The wiring harness will sometimes interfere with the oil pan as it's lowered onto the case, so make sure that it is as snug to the valve body as possible. There are also several clamps that will locate and

hold down the harness. Because the plastic sleeve is new, it may not want to go into place easily.

We also found that the harness wanted to go under our crossover tube, which on the early models has a different routing that does not interfere with the wiring harness. Make sure to have positive engagement with all electrical components.

Installing a New Wiring Harness

1 *Any rebuild kit should come with a new wiring harness, as ours did from Monster Transmission. The new harness will be stiff and require some cajoling to fit in place properly.*

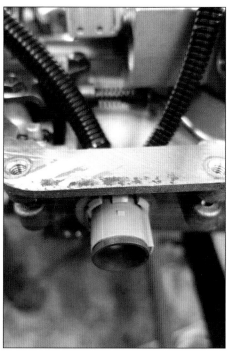

2 Denny suggested throwing some assembly lube on the O-ring for the external connector. It will help the stiff plastic and O-ring combination seat more easily.

3 There's not much room to push the connector through, which is why assembly lube was used. The plastic can be brittle, so avoid using anything too hard to pry it into place. It will snap into place when seated correctly.

4 Our connector only needed a deft touch, and it pressed into place. We do not recommend reusing old wiring harnesses. It's too easy for an old O-ring to leak or, worse, have a bad connection resulting in the unit not functioning.

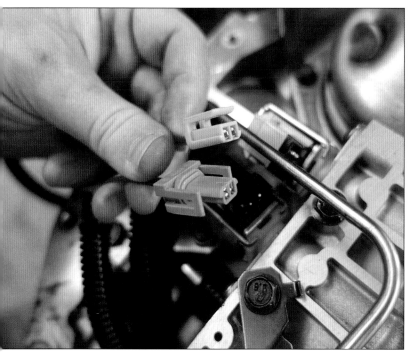

5 There are two unique plugs for the shift solenoids. It is virtually impossible to install them incorrectly.

6 Wiring harnesses are different for the different model years. This one has the temperature sensor built into the wiring harness. Older models will have the temperature sensor located near the front of the case embedded in the valve body.

7 *Our weather pack connectors are snapped securely in place, and the wires are given enough slack so that they do not bind.*

8 *There are two more connections near the front of the case: one for the PWM solenoid (grey clip) and the variable-force motor (white clip). Note the clamp holding down the harness with a bolt through the valve body.*

9 *Removing the crossover tube and feeding the wiring harness under it provided more clearance when we reinstalled the transmission pan.*

10 *Once more, snug down the retaining clip.*

Temperature Sensor Differences

Early models have a built-in temperature sensor in the valve body, while the late models have a fluid temperature sensor built into the harness, which looks like a terminated and zip-tied node. Both versions are valid. ■

This is the filter neck seal. A tight seal here will make sure the filter doesn't leak internally into the case.

The wiring harness only installs one way, and the connections are pretty self-explanatory when the harness is laid out. Confirm that the harness is snug to the valve body so that the oil filter has room to be affixed correctly.

Oil Filter

Now that you're on the home stretch, the oil filter neck seal can be replaced if it hasn't already been done. The oil filter itself is press fit into place in only one orientation. Once you start pressing the oil filter into place, you'll most likely feel the wiring harness compress and crack a little.

If the oil filter does not fully seat or sit level with the case, rearrange the

Installing the New Oil Filter

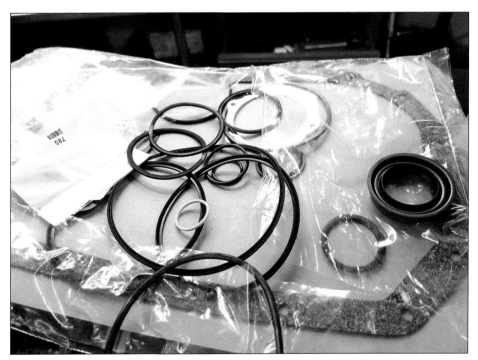

1 *This is a standard rebuild kit with a cork pan gasket and a host of new gaskets and seals. Upgraded kits like ours from Monster Transmission come with better seals and gaskets in most cases.*

2 *A new transmission pan filter neck is installed and comes with a basic install kit.*

3 *Denny presses a new oil filter into place and is ready for a dry fit of the oil pan.*

4 *The filter should fit snug in its receptacle.*

harness because the filter will need room under the oil pan. We had to wiggle the wiring harness a few times to get everything to fit properly. It will eventually be rerouted slightly to make sure the filter fit well.

Pan Gasket

Once the filter is situated, lay the pan gasket into place. Some kits come with cork gaskets, and some of the more expensive versions have a steel-impregnated rubberized version. We went with the upgraded version.

Installing the Pan Gasket

1 *Less-expensive kits have a cork pan gasket. Since it's no longer the 1980s and technology has improved, we opted for the rubber gasket with impregnated washers that came with the Monster Transmission kit.*

2 *Denny dry fits the pan for clearance. There shouldn't be any need to press hard or force anything down.*

3 *During the dry fit, the wiring harness was bound up around the filter and a few things needed to be moved around. You do not want the filter pressed against the pan.*

The original gasket is a controlled-compression type of gasket and can be reused, assuming that nothing was broken or ripped in the original gasket. We always opt for replacing this gasket when possible just for the sake of knowing that it's in good working order. If you removed the oil-pan magnet, make sure to put it back now.

Now, lower the pan onto the case and check for fitment. The pan will lower onto the pan gasket easily without having to smash the pan to fit. The filter can touch the pan, but it should not be forced. We had to wiggle the filter into a new position once or twice to get the suitable fitting. Once you are happy with your oil pan, install the 17 black flanged head pan bolts and torque to 18 ft-lbs. For all of the GM4L80E torque specifications, see the Appendix.

Congratulations! You have completed your rebuild.

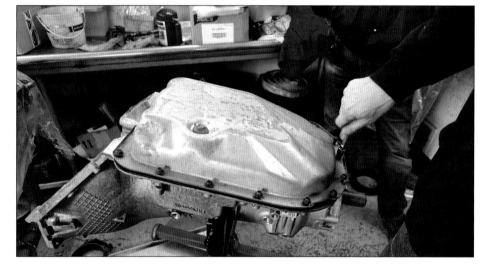

We hand tightened all the bolts and went back to torque them down to 18 ft-lbs.

There is one longer pan bolt that is different from the rest because it secures the dipstick tube between the case molding. This slot often holds the cable housing bracket.

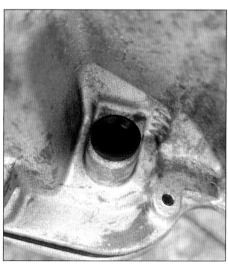

A rebuild kit will come with a dipstick tube gasket. Replace it for cheap insurance.

TROUBLESHOOTING

Troubleshooting refers to discovering a problem and being able to correctly identify its cause. This helps with fixing the error or component. This chapter deals with common issues that often plague the 4L80E internally and externally.

This adage applies: "an ounce of prevention is worth a pound of cure." While many regard doing a full transmission fluid flush every year to be overcautious, it has been mentioned many times by the builders of these units. Although it is more than what the factory recommended, they saw evidence that a simple fluid change on a regular basis can extend the life of the transmission. It may even result in tens of thousands or even hundreds of thousands of miles of longevity.

While the 4L80E is a formidable transmission, it is not entirely devoid of issues. If it were perfect, GM would not have updated it during the transmission's life cycle. Over time, components that were designed to wear down will eventually deteriorate and need to be replaced, which should be expected with any moving mechanical part.

Wear particles from clutch packs, metal dust, and old oil ends up in places that cause damage. Driver abuse from towing, racing, or neglect adds up over time. All of this can culminate in the downfall of the 4L80E—just as it can with any transmission, which can be evidenced by leaks, squeaks, rattles, missed shifts, no shifts, or ultimate failure of the unit itself.

Troubleshooting is more challenging now that computers have entered the picture. In many ways, computers have both simplified and complicated the life of automobile ownership. Fortunately, there have been millions of 4L80Es on the road and more than two decades of experiences from owners and repair facilities that help to anticipate many of these common problems and accurately diagnose issues.

In this chapter, information has been gathered to address as many common and perhaps not-so-common issues that may arise during the operation of the 4L80E. Many fixes can be performed while the transmission is still in the car, but others require full removal of the

unit. Before tearing into a project, begin diagnosing an issue by evaluating things that can be observed.

The good news is that modern transmission and drivetrain problems can often be solved with a few basic items before major teardown occurs. First, check the following:

- Fluid level is too high or too low
- A transmission error code is being shown
- The engine is running poorly or having some impact on drivability
- The shift linkage or cable is out of alignment or stretched
- A sensor has failed and needs replacing
- The TCU has failed or is not communicating with the ECU
- The transmission is leaking
- The driveshaft is out of balance
- The transmission oil needs flushed

After these first items have been evaluated and determined to not be the cause, then it is prudent to continuing to explore further down the rabbit hole.

Trouble Chart	
Symptom	**Potential Causes and Repairs**

Delayed 1-2 shift	1. The output speed sensor has a bad connection, bad wiring, a poor signal, or a failed unit.
	2. The input speed sensor has a bad connection, bad wiring, a poor signal, or a failed unit.
	3. The PSM has a bad connection, bad wiring, a poor signal, or a failed unit.
	4. Incorrect PROM calibration.
	5. Possible fault codes:
	    a. 24 – Output speed sensor
	    b. 28 – PSM
	    c. 85 – Undefined ratio

Engine stalling	1. The forward clutch housing bearing is seized. 2. The fourth clutch components are seized or jammed. 3. The overrun clutch components are seized or jammed. 4. The torque converter clutch (TCC) is stuck on or is dragging. Rebuild the TCC in the valve body.
Engine starts in gear	1. Check and replace the neutral safety switch. 2. The manual shift valve is not engaged to detent level or is stuck in the wrong position. 3. Check for the proper alignment with the shifter cable.

First and second gears only	1. Solenoid B is stuck in the off position or there is a loose connection or a broken wire.
	2. There is no PCM signal to Solenoid B.
	3. The 2-3 shift valve is stuck or damaged.
	4. There is QDM failure.
	5. Possible error codes:
	    a. 68 – Overdrive ratio
	    b. 81 – QDM and solenoid B faults
	    c. 85 – Undefined ratio
	    d. 87 – Solenoid B stuck off

Foaming fluid	1. There is contaminated transmission oil from anti-freeze in the radiator. 2. The engine overheated. 3. The vehicle overloaded.
Forward movement in neutral gear	1. The manual valve is stuck or mispositioned. 2. The shift cable stretched and needs to be replaced. 3. The shift cable is misaligned and needs adjustment. 4. The forward clutch seized and jammed. 5. The hub holes are plugged.

Trouble Chart	
Symptom	**Potential Causes and Repairs**

Hard to shift	1. The line pressure is too high or too low.
	2. The force motor has a bad connection, bad wiring, a poor signal, or a failed unit.
	3. The PCM has a bad connection, bad wiring, a poor signal, or a failed unit.
	4. The accumulator piston is leaking or stuck.
	5. The check balls are missing.
	6. The PROM calibration is incorrect.
	7. Possible fault codes:
	    a. 21 – TPS high
	    b. 22 – TPS low
	    c. 24 – Output speed
	    d. 28 – PSM
	    e. 53 – System voltage high
	    f. 68 – Overdrive ratio
	    g. 73 – Force motor current
	    h. 75 – System voltage low
	    i. 81 – QDM and solenoid B
	    j. 85 – Undefined ratio

Hard to shift from drive to reverse	1. The direct lube oil passage is blocked. 2. There is a forward clutch spring malfunction. 3. The check balls are stuck.
Hard to shift out of park	1. The vehicle is parked on a hill. 2. The parking pawl return spring is weak or broken.
High line pressure	1. Replace the pressure regulator valve. 2. Replace the reverse boost valve. 3. Check for loose connections at the PCM or the force motor. 4. Check for broken components in the valve body.

Inaccurate shift points	1. The output speed sensor has a bad connection, bad wiring, a poor signal, or a failed unit.
	2. The throttle position sensor has a bad connection, bad wiring, a poor signal, or a failed unit.
	3. The PSM has a bad connection, bad wiring, a poor signal, or a failed unit.
	4. The axle ratio changed from the original.
	5. The tire size changed from the original.
	6. There is digital radio adapter failure (2WD units only).
	7. Possible fault codes:
	    a. 21 – TPS high
	    b. 22 – TPS low
	    c. 24 – Output speed sensor
	    d. 28 – PSM
	    e. 85 – Undefined ratio

Loss of forward drive	1. There is torque converter failure. 2. It is low on oil. 3. There is a seized or broken oil pump. 4. There is a broken roller clutch or carrier. 5. The turbine shaft is broken or has sheared splines. 6. The forward clutch components are broken, worn, or not seated properly. 7. The reverse gearset is broken.

Trouble Chart	
Symptom	**Potential Causes and Repairs**
Low line pressure	1. The oil pump is worn, broken, or has a bad seal between the body to case or the case gasket. 2. The pressure regulator valve is stuck due to debris. 3. The reverse booster is stuck due to debris. 4. The oil pump valve is worn and damaged. 5. There are leaks within the valve body itself or the gaskets. 6. The force motor may be broken or stuck in the on position. 7. Possible PCM failure with force motor PCM codes showing.
No engine braking	1. There is main shaft damage. 2. There is output shaft damage. 3. The oil pressure is low or has low oil level. 4. The rear band assembly is not seated. 5. The check ball is missing, broken, or inappropriately sized. 6. There is bushing or thrust washer wear or damage. 7. The reverse servo piston, seal, cover, gasket, or bolt need to be inspected for wear or damage. 8. The direct clutch housing splines are worn or the outer band is worn or damaged. 9. The valve body and/or bolts are broken or cracked.
No first gear	1. Inspect the gear selector assembly and cable. 2. The detent level inside the transmission is misaligned. 3. There is case damage or the rear band is broken or loose. 4. The roller assembly is broken. 5. The center support is broken or not supported. 6. There is damage to the sun gear. 7. Input and output speed sensors are giving no readings.

No fourth gear	1. The fourth clutch components are damaged (seals, bolt loose/broken, cup plug missing, piston, spring assembly, snap ring or clutch plates are damaged).
	2. There is damage to the fourth clutch housing itself.
	3. The overrun housing components are broken, worn, or damaged, such as the sun gear, housing, or clutch plates.
	4. Solenoid B is stuck off or there is a broken wire, poor connection, or voltage failure.
	5. There is PCM failure.
	6. There is quad driver module (QDM) failure.
	7. Potential fault codes:
	   a. 21 – TPS High
	   b. 22 – TPS low
	   c. 28 – PSM fault
	   d. 68 – Overdrive ratio
	   e. 75 – System voltage low
	   f. 81 – QDM and solenoid B fault

Trouble Chart	
Symptom	**Potential Causes and Repairs**
No movement in gear	1. Check for low oil. 2. The TCC may be stuck. 3. Check for a loose connector. 4. There may be debris in the fluid or the torque converter. 5. Possible damage to the stator shaft, the turbine shaft, the main shaft, or the output shaft.
No overrun braking	1. Inspect the PSM for wiring issues, a loose connector, or no signal. 2. The clutch plates are worn or broken. 3. The output shaft splines are damaged. 4. The seals or check balls are leaking. 5. The sun gear is worn or damaged. 6. The oil passages are blocked. 7. The overrun housing, piston, or spring are not functioning properly.
No parking gear	1. The detent lever is misaligned internally or via the shift linkage. 2. The actuator rod is bent or broken. 3. The parking pawl or parking pawl shaft is broken. 4. The manual shift shaft is misaligned.
No reverse gear	1. There is low oil or low oil pressure. 2. The check balls are missing in the valve body. 3. The rear band anchor pin is broken or the rear band is not aligned properly. 4. The center support or center support seal is leaking. 5. The center support bolt is loose or leaking. 6. The rear band is broken or installed improperly. 7. The direct clutch friction discs or plates are worn or broken. 8. The direct clutch housing, piston, or seals are leaking or worn excessively.
No second gear	1. The front band assembly anchor pin is broken or in the incorrect position. 2. The intermediate clutch feed cup plug is missing or leaking. 3. The intermediate clutch components are broken, missing, or worn. 4. The improper fluid was used. 5. The intermediate sprag is broken or worn. 6. The direct clutch housing or snap ring was improperly installed or broken.

Trouble Chart

Symptom	Potential Causes and Repairs

No third gear	1. The front band is stuck in the on position.
	 2. The direct clutch assembly is leaking, broken, worn, or damaged. The seals, piston, housing, spring assembly, and clutch plates require inspection.
	 3. The center support assembly is leaking at the case or the broken center support bolt.
	 4. The direct clutch support bolt is loose, leaking, or broken.
	 5. Solenoid B is stuck in the off position or has a broken wire, O-ring damage, or part failure.
	 6. The 2-3 shift valve is stuck or broken.
	 7. There is PCM failure.
	 8. Related fault codes:
	    a. 81 – Quad driver module (QDM) and solenoid B fault
	    b. 85 – Undefined ratio
	    c. 87 – Solenoid B stuck off

No torque converter clutch (TCC)	1. The TCC solenoid has a fault, there is O-ring failure, or there is no wiring connection or voltage to the solenoid.
	 2. There is quad driver module failure.
	 3. There is TCC valve failure often due to debris or sediment buildup.
	 4. There is torque converter failure.
	 5. There are plugged oil galleys in the turbine shaft or worn shaft seals.
	 6. The oil pump bushing is worn or damaged.
	 7. The regulated apply valve is stuck open or closed.
	 8. The TCC valve release exhaust orifice is blocked.
	 9. Possible fault codes:
	    a. 21 – TPS high
	    b. 22 – TPS low
	    c. 28 – PSM fault
	    d. 37 – Brake switch stuck on
	    e. 39 – TCC stuck off
	    f. 53 – System voltage too high
	    g. 68 – Overdrive ratio
	    h. 75 – QDM and solenoid B fault
	    i. 83 – QDM and TCC solenoid faults

No torque in second gear	1. The intermediate sprag has failed or has excessive eccentricity.
Noise from the 4L80E	1. The torque converter bolts are loose, out of balance, or had a failure. 2. The engine and transmission are in misalignment. 3. The output shaft bearings and support are worn out.
Not able to shift D2 to D1	1. The rear band is broken or worn out. 2. The detent level has poor travel or is worn. 3. The shift cable is in misalignment.
Not able to shift D3 to D2	1. There is front band failure.

Trouble Chart

Symptom	Potential Causes and Repairs
Not able to shift out of park	1. The actuator rod is broken or stretched. 2. The linkage is damaged or broken.
Oil coming out of the breather	1. The pump cover cross channels are leaking. 2. There is foaming fluid or the transmission is overfilled. 3. The transmission overheated.
Shift lever shows incorrect gear	1. A misaligned indicator linkage needs adjusting. 2. The manual valve body is not engaging with the detent lever; the detent is misaligned or broken. 3. The manual shift shaft is not aligned properly.
Shift selector lever finds no gear	1. The detent lever is loose or broken. 2. The manual valve body is stuck and potentially has blockage. 3. The valve body has debris within the channels.
Soft shift from drive to reverse	1. The direct oil feed passage is blocked. 2. The direct clutch oil is blocked.
Soft shifts	1. The line pressure is too low. 2. The force motor has a bad connection, bad wiring, a poor signal, or a failed unit. 3. There is PCM failure. 4. There is an accumulator piston or spring malfunction. 5. The PROM is incorrectly calibrated. 6. Possible fault code: a. 73 – Force motor current
Starts in fourth gear	1. Solenoid B is stuck on or has failed wiring. 2. Possible fault code: a. 86 – Solenoid B stuck on
Starts in second gear	1. The intermediate clutch plates have seized. 2. The direct clutch lube feed is blocked. 3. The center support springs or piston are jammed. 4. There is solenoid A failure or O-ring failure. 5. There is PCM signal to solenoid failure. 6. QDM failed. 7. The 1-2 shift valve is stuck. 8. Possible fault code: a. 82 QDM and solenoid A.
Starts in third gear	1. The forward driving hub is plugged or has seized pressure plates. 2. The direct clutch components failed or seized.

Trouble Chart	
Symptom	**Potential Causes and Repairs**

TCC applying at the wrong time	1. The output speed sensor has a bad connection, bad wiring, a poor signal, or a failed unit.
	2. The throttle position sensor has bad wiring, a bad connection, or a failed unit.
	3. PCM failure.
	4. The PSM has a bad connection, bad wiring, or a failed unit.
	5. The transmission temperature sensor has bad wiring, a bad connection, or a failed unit.
	6. The engine coolant temperature sensor has bad wiring, a bad connection, or a failed unit.
	7. The brake switch has bad wiring, a bad connection, or a failed unit.
	8. There is a digital radio adapter malfunction (2WD only).
	9. Possible fault codes:
	   a. 14 – Engine temperature sensor high
	   b. 15 – Engine temperature sensor low
	   c. 21 – TPS sensor high
	   d. 22 – TPS sensor low
	   e. 24 – Output speed sensor
	   f. 28 – PSM
	   g. 58 – Transmission temperature sensor high
	   h. 59 – Transmission temperature sensor low
	   i. 68 – Overdrive ratio

TCC stuck on	1. There is TCC gasket failure. 2. There is TCC solenoid failure. 3. The TCC wiring is faulty. 4. The TCC apply valve is stuck. 5. QDM failure. 6. Possible fault code: a. 83 – QDM and TCC solenoid fault
Transmission fluid overheating	1. Possible debris blockage in the TCC oil passages or a broken TCC spring. 2. The oil pump cover has internal leakage. 3. The pressure regulator valve is locked on high. 4. The oil cooler airflow is blocked at the cooler or the cooler lines have blockage. 5. There is potential damage to internal retainer pins or gaskets. 6. The turbine shaft seal or O-ring is damaged or broken. 7. The stator shaft bushing has damage or wear. 8. The oil transfer hole cup plug is leaking or broken. 9. There is low fluid level. 10. There is poor airflow to the radiator and/or blockage.

Trouble Chart	
Symptom	**Potential Causes and Repairs**
Transmission seized	1. The rear lubrication components seized, are blocked, or are jammed. 2. The valve body is loose or broken. 3. There is a blocked main filter. 4. The output shaft seal lube holes are missing or damaged. 5. The main shaft lube holes are missing. 6. The center support lube holes are missing. 7. The center support is not held properly. 8. The rear band or servo is locked (seized in second, third, or fourth only).
Transmission slipping	1. The fluid level is too high or too low.
Vibrations	1. The torque converter is out of balance or in failure. 2. The transmission and engine are out of alignment to frame. 3. The output shaft seals or bearings are worn. 4. There is worn stator shaft surface at the turbine shaft. 5. The main shaft has excessive wear. 6. The output shaft has excessive wear.
Weak TCC apply	1. The turbine shaft seals are worn. 2. The pump body bushings are worn. 3. Leaking oil transfer holes. 4. There is TCC solenoid failure. 5. There is low transmission oil fluid or pressure. 6. The TCC valve release is blocked.
Will not stay in park position	1. The manual detent spring is broken, loose, or weak.

Common Failures

Overheating is a common failure. The plastic cage that holds the overdrive roller clutch can melt, which causes instant death of the transmission. In extreme conditions, such as snow plowing, it is advised to use the manual D-1-2 setting so that the overdrive roller clutch is being support by the overrun clutch, which will provide engine braking and help distribute the load onto the overrun clutch over the roller clutch more evenly. Do not use overdrive when using it under loads.

Sonnax overrun has a kit to fix this (part number 34200-40K).

APPENDIX

GM 4L80E Transmission Torque Specs			
Description	**Nm**	**Ft-lbs**	**In-lbs**
Solenoid to valve body screw	8	–	71
Control valve assembly to case screw	11	–	97
Oil test hole plug	11	–	97
Flywheel housing cover to transmission screw	7	–	62
Pump body to cover screw	24	18	–
Pump assembly to case screw	24	18	–
Rear servo cover to case screw	24	18	–
Pressure control solenoid bracket to valve body	8	–	71
Parking pawl bracket to case screw	24	18	–
Accumulator housing to valve body screw	11	–	97
Fourth clutch screw	16	12	–
Pan to case screw	24	18	–
Extension housing to case screw	34	25	–
Manual shaft to detent lever nut	24	18	–
Speed sensor to case screw	11	–	97
Case center support screw	39	29	–
Flywheel to converter screw	44	32	–
Transmission case to engine screw	44	32	–
Cooler pipe connector nut at case and radiator	38	28	–
Valve body-to-case lube pipe	11	–	97
Engine rear mount to transmission bolt	44	32	–
Engine rear support bracket to frame nut	44	32	–
Valve body to case PSM	11	–	97
Oil pan drain plug	34	25	–